# A Therapist's Guide to Mapping
# the Girl Heroine's Journey in Sandplay

# A Therapist's Guide to Mapping the Girl Heroine's Journey in Sandplay

Rosalind Heiko

Foreword by Eric J. Green

ROWMAN & LITTLEFIELD
Lanham • Boulder • New York • London

Published by Rowman & Littlefield
A wholly owned subsidiary of The Rowman & Littlefield Publishing Group, Inc.
4501 Forbes Boulevard, Suite 200, Lanham, Maryland 20706
www.rowman.com

Unit A, Whitacre Mews, 26-34 Stannary Street, London SE11 4AB

British Library Cataloguing in Publication Information Available

**Library of Congress Cataloging-in-Publication Data**

Names: Heiko, Rosalind, author.
Title: A therapist's guide to mapping the girl heroine's journey in sandplay / Rosalind Heiko ;
    foreword by Eric Green.
Description: Lanham : Rowman & Littlefield, [2018] | Includes bibliographical references
    and index.
Identifiers: LCCN 2018005794 (print) | LCCN 2018007134 (ebook) | ISBN 9781538116609
    (Electronic) | ISBN 9781442253810 (cloth) | ISBN 9781538116593 (pbk.)
Subjects: | MESH: Mental Disorders—therapy | Play Therapy—methods | Child | Women—
    psychology | Case Reports
Classification: LCC RJ505.P6 (ebook) | LCC RJ505.P6 (print) | NLM WS 350.4 | DDC
    618.92/891653—dc23
LC record available at https://lccn.loc.gov/2018005794

This book is dedicated to my amazing adult children:
the son and daughter I birthed and the daughter of my heart,
married to my son. And now, at this writing,
to Noah, our fierce and sweet grandchild.

Above all, be the heroine of your life, not the victim. . . . It will be a little messy, but embrace the mess. It will be complicated, but rejoice in the complications. It will not be anything like what you think it will be like, but surprises are good for you. And don't be frightened: you can always change your mind.

Nora Ephron, Wellesley College Commencement Speech 1996
http://www.wellesley.edu/events/commencement/
archives/1996commencement


Let the beauty we love be what we do.

Rumi, from "A Great Wagon"
Translated by Coleman Barks


Never grow a wishbone, daughter, where your backbone ought to be.

J. Paddleford
*Hometown Appetites: The Story of Clementine Paddleford,*
*the Forgotten Food Writer Who Chronicled How America Ate*

~

# Contents

~

# Foreword

**Nishi:** This is a stone called *"beryl."* Try peeking into the crack.
**Shizuku:** Ohhh! It's so pretty!
**Nishi:** It's called "beryl." There's an inclusion of raw emerald.
**Shizuku:** Emerald? The gemstone?
**Nishi:** That's right. You're like that stone, the beryl. Unpolished stones in their natural state. Now, I like even unpolished stones very much. You have to find the rough gems inside yourself, take the time, and polish them. It's very time-consuming work. That rock has a largest stone, right?
**Shizuku:** Yes.
**Nishi:** Actually, that one, when you polish it, instead turns out to be worthless. The smaller ones further inside are of higher purity. And in a part, you can't see from the outside, there might be even better stones.
**Shizuku:** I've become very afraid of finding out whether or not I have a beautiful crystal or beryl like this inside me. But I want to write. When I've written my story, I'll be sure to show it to you first.
**Nishi:** Thank you.

This opening dialogue was adapted from Academy Award-winning Japanese director Hayao Miyazaki's 2005 anime feature, *Whispers of the Heart*. Shizuku, the film's adolescent protagonist, is seeking answers in her life as she finds herself with a new, nascent love interest, as well as she begins to explore what may be a long-term passion and skill as a creative writer. She seeks the wisdom and comfort of Nishi, her friend's grandfather, who uses the story of polishing the *beryl*, or emerald gemstone, as a metaphor for finding the psychological treasure within. This coming-of-age tale, including the oftentimes scary and alien process for a teen, mainly of looking inward as opposed to outward for acceptance, is analogous to the great feminine journey afforded through sandplay and illuminated in Rosalind Heiko's new book, *A Therapist's Guide to Mapping the Girl Heroine's Journey in Sandplay*.

Several years ago, I was advised by a mutual colleague and well-known author in play therapy, to seek out Dr. Heiko for guidance or consultation about joining the sandplay parent organization here in the United States, the Sandplay Therapists of America (STA). I attended her talk in Dallas, Texas, on fairy tales and archetypal themes in sandplay. And I was quite captured by her wholehearted joy when describing sandplay case material, her eloquence in illuminating the heroine's journey through sand, and her valorization of the seminal importance of Kalff's "free and protected space," which has stayed with me all these years later. "The child experiences, quite unconsciously, what I call a free and at the same time, a protected space" (Kalff*, 1980, p. 39). Dr. Heiko continues to highlight the theme of the free and protected space (i.e., keeping a child's psychological work in therapy free from judgement and protected from psychological intrusions) throughout her current work in this text. It is the cogent condition upon which healing may stem from within the co-transference afforded by sandplay. So what is sandplay, exactly, and why is this book worth reading?

First, sandplay, as a psychotherapeutic modality, is almost unknown outside the mental health community. Quite simply, it's the child's use of miniatures to create sand pictures in a sand tray within a consulting room. The Kalffian approach, the modality in which Dr. Heiko and I have been trained through STA, is non-directive, does not encourage interpretation by therapists to children of the potential meaning of their sandplay, and is hallmarked by therapists undergoing their own personal analysis, often for many years, to minimize opportunities of polluting the child's therapy by not projecting their own inner turmoil into the process.

Sandplay, as an organic, enjoyable pastime at the beach, has been a fun tradition for children over many years, especially during annual holidays to the coast when children accompany their families to the sea to relax and play. What makes sandplay in a consulting room inherently different or healing from typical sandplay and building sandcastles at the beach, is that in this sandplay, a trained adult holds and contains the space for the child to do the necessary inner work. In this therapeutic holding or embracing the child's psychological warts and all without judgement, self-led healing often emerges within children as their sense of self-understanding and their understanding of themselves in relation to others may begin to qualitatively improve.

Rosalind Heiko is a nationally recognized sandplay expert who has masterfully woven mythology, interpersonal biology, mysticism, feminism, spirituality, child-centered play therapy, and Jungian interpretation throughout her text. She not only simplifies the complex process of sandplay with children but also provides a practical tool, a map or guide, based in part on Betty Jackson's seminal work in this area, to interpret or analyze, children's sand pictures, that many mental health practitioners will find accessible to use in sandplay and valuable when extracting meaning.

---

*Kalff, D. (1980). *Sandplay: A Psychotherapeutic Approach to the Psyche*. Santa Monica, CA: Sigo Press.

She dedicates an entire section of her book on counseling LGBTQ youth and the compassion and understanding required to sensitively care for this specialized, often misunderstood, group. She includes two in-depth case studies, which exemplify her sandplay approaches with children, from the Kalffian tradition, and highlights the great feminine journey afforded through the sandplay process. And what better person from us to learn about the mystical meaning in sandplay and the great feminine or *mother* archetype, as Erich Neumann taught us, than from a woman, who by her accounts at the beginning of the book, describes her own heroic journey throughout childhood and overcoming obstacles and impediments at every turn, sometimes even from those very adults entrusted with her care.

Her writing style demonstrates how she is uniquely and manifestly qualified to narrate the soulful beauty inherent within sandplay: she exudes humble confidence through her many forays through the text of amplifying tenets of sandplay and her patients' journeys through myth and meaning. For example, read the David Whyte poem she cites: it's evocative, spellbinding, and mercurial. By the end of the book, I found myself going back to read it a second time, to ensure I had digested the many lessons that I would need not to write this foreword, but to improve upon my own clinical work with traumatized children in the consulting room. Yes, it's that good. And yes, I highly recommend its careful, mindful, and deliberate reading to afford reflection, and ultimate resonating.

At the conclusion of *Whispers of the Heart*, Shizuku informs Nishi, who surprisingly gifted her the valuable emerald encrusted stone, that she will start chipping away and polishing the beryl soon. Nishi retorts that she has already begun the process by initiating the journey and being brave in the land of the living. Similarly, Dr. Heiko, toward the end of her book, states, "When we choose to face our fears, to reach for more, we become stronger, clearer and highly engaged in living fully. Sandplay makes the journey bearable and allows our hearts to open to what is possible for us in each moment." Thank you, for encouraging us all, from seasoned clinician to novice beginner, to join with you, to look inside our own beryl, face our fears, and trust in the process that we will all come out better in the end, as well our patients, who we join in this special, life-affirming, sand-based journey of care and compassion. May we all strive to be brave, as Dr. Heiko tacitly reminds us by demonstrating the archetype of the *wounded healer*, to never lose sight of hope and our eternal sense of childlike wonder.

Eric J. Green, Ph.D.
Johns Hopkins University
February 2018

~

# Preface

A long time ago, a little girl with red hair and freckles was playing by herself near her mother with her new bucket and shovel at the beach. Seeing another little girl playing a short distance away, she realized that she wanted to make a new friend. She asked her mother to come with her and help introduce her. Her mother said firmly: "Daughter, take a deep breath, square your shoulders, and do it yourself." So she did. She made a new friend, using her own resources and strength—with her mother's blessing and love.

She took that deep breath . . . after her sister was born and went through many hospitalizations. And then when her mother went in for the first of many hospital stays.

She took that deep breath . . . when the father that she idolized began to disappear from family times without explanation.

She took that deep breath . . . when two girls named Mary and Nancy refused to play with her in fourth grade and wouldn't tell her why, even when she ran after them and begged to know.

She took that deep breath . . . when her mother, wrecked by internal and external suffering, slapped and screamed at her and her sister and drove away from their house, saying she was never coming back—over and over.

She took that deep breath . . . when she sang her first solo in chorus, and later in recitals and school musicals, the times she could let her voice soar.

She took that deep breath . . . when the girl she thought was her best friend in middle school stopped talking to her because the girl's mother said it wasn't good to be friends with a Jew.

She took that deep breath . . . when her parents fought and screamed and finally divorced.

She took that deep breath . . . when her high school creative writing teacher told her to stop fooling around with writing science fiction and, instead, write serious fiction—whatever that meant.

She took that deep breath . . . when her mother told her never to share "family business" with outsiders after the guidance counselor the girl spoke to about family concerns immediately called her mother about the meeting.

She took that deep breath . . . when she realized that the woman her father remarried was a damaged forever child herself, addicted to alcohol and dramatic angry scenes.

She took that deep breath . . . and fixed the memories in her mind of laughing so deeply with her mother that it hurt her sides and lightened her heart.

She took that deep breath . . . when Father Curley, one of her professors at St. John's University, told her not to pursue a doctorate, because she'd likely drop out and have babies and should leave an opening for a qualified male candidate instead. So she left that school, and went to Syracuse University, where she had the time of her life, personally and professionally. And received her doctorate.

She took that deep breath . . . and vowed never to marry or have children. And broke that vow after she met a man who looked just like her idea of just right—and ended up having two children with him.

She took that deep breath . . . and fully heard the conference organizer tell her that hers was the worst talk the organizer ever heard anyone give. And after the blast of shame receded, proceeded to remake herself into the best speaker and trainer she possibly could. Because truth matters (maybe kindness too, the girl decided, maybe compassion is a necessary part of sharing truth).

She took that deep breath . . . and rode the back seat of an ambulance one day many years ago with her own daughter, one of many such trips. And realized that wherever this ride took her, and them—it would be okay, because they had created a web of love and friendship to support and hold them at its heart.

The bravest children I know work in sand, as part of integrated therapeutic treatment. The term *integrative therapy* describes "the syntheses of theory and skill to best meet a client's needs from a holistic perspective" (Green, 2014, p.162). Sandplay is the foremost among many treatment modalities I employ to alleviate client difficulties and challenges, one that can be described as self-directed trauma play as well.

Parents bring their daughters into my office waiting room, after first having met with me in a previous session. They discuss what they believe their child needs to learn for herself, as well as what concerns they have for her well-being. When the parents or guardians bring the child in, I state that when the child walks down the short corridor into my office suite with her family, she will find two pathways marked by doorways, representative of that "fork at the end of a road" to which Yogi Berra once referred (2001, p.1). I suggest that she pick a doorway, and walk through. The girls generally stop at the end of the hall. To each side are door frames with open access to each room. Each girl then chooses which way she will step. Turning to the left leads to my family consulting room with couch and chairs. Moving to the right leads to the sandplay / play therapy room. Sometimes it takes more than a few seconds for the girls to choose which doorway to go through. I explain that it is fine to take all the time needed in order to make this decision.

This choice will be the first of many the clients will take in relation to their therapeutic process. If the girl is unable to decide where to move, this may prove more than a bit uncomfortable for her and sometimes can make her parents quite uneasy. A calm, relaxed stance on my part helps to hold this initial and vital part of the girl's heroine's journey. Will she ask her parents to choose? If she turns left and sits, tentatively, on the couch next to one of her parents, I wonder: Will she be willing to take up the space she deserves? If she marches into the play room and begins to touch the sand, I wonder: How has life begun to mold this child? True to my training, both in clinical hypnosis and the Buddhist practice to which I was introduced years ago in my sandplay training in Switzerland with Martin Kalff, I remain alert and curious about the next steps. Each personal journey is unique in symbolic or abstract expression in the sand and in play. And yet . . . the sandplay journey leads these girls through an understandable process that can be mapped visually.

This book is organized into six parts. In order to more fully engage with an understanding of mapping the young feminine journey, the traditions and essential practices of sandplay are clarified. Part I relates the background of the concept of the journey with relation to heroine and hero archetypal mapping. In part II, the clinical process of sandplay—the history, essential features, an explanation of sandplay as fitting into the context of integrative child therapy, the notion of co-transference, previous models of the sandplay journey, and a look at one parent's perspective of how sandplay positively affected her daughter's emotional development are addressed. Part II also contains an exploration of the use of the mandala in mapping the journey, and provides an illustration and interpretation for each of the aspects of the Sandplay Journey Map. Part III examines the use of the fairy tale "Vasilisa the Brave" in amplifying our understanding of how the Sandplay Journey Map can be applied to mapping the girl's quintessential journey in the sand. Part IV demonstrates how the trays of the children "Lainey" and "Jess" can be employed with the Sandplay Journey Map in clinical practice. Part V considers the Sandplay Journey Map in relation to individual and group consultation experiences, and how to handle clinical mistakes that become apparent after applying the Journey Map in case review. The conclusions in part VI suggest that the use of the Sandplay Journey Map represents a means of strengthening our clinical acuity and overall perspective on both individual casework and our general understanding of the complexities of clinical dynamics with regard to the journey of girls.

Back to that summer's day at the beach. What did the girl want? She wanted the adventure of meeting someone new. She wanted to have a good time. She wanted connection, fun, friendship, play, laughter, and the joy of building something together. She wanted all the things that make life satisfying and "juicy" and full of promise—the things that are gifted through this Great Adventure we call life here on earth. The girl learned persistence. She decided that endeavoring to reach for more was worth the effort. So she took those steps across the sand.

This book is dedicated to the courageous girls with whom I've worked all these years. Every girl, whether the life is long or short, goes through her own heroine's journey. A journey that is composed in part of great beauty, determination, vulnerability, risk, and sacrifice. My mother's advice is free: Take a deep breath, square your shoulders, and begin.

~

# Acknowledgments

I want to thank the following publishers and authors/translators for permission to quote and reprint material for this book:

"Alcestis on the Poetry Circuit" © 1973, 2015 by Erica Mann Jong. Reprinted with permission of the poet.

Coleman Barks. "A Great Wagon" by Rumi. Reprinted with permission of Mr. Barks.

"Mystery" from *My Grandfather's Blessings: Stories of Strength, Refuge, and Belonging* by Rachel Naomi Remen, M.D. © 2000. Used by permission of Riverhead, an imprint of Penguin Publishing Group, a division of Penguin Random House LLC.

"Start Close In" © 2012 by David Whyte. Reprinted with permission of the poet.

"The Journey" © 1997 by David Whyte. Reprinted with permission of the poet.

Jacob Nordby from *Blessed Are the Weird*. Reprinted with permission of the author.

I'd like to express my gratitude to Mark Golding (http://markgolding.co.uk/), Soul Alchemist Extraordinaire, who worked his magic and created the Sandplay Journey Map illustration; and to Sharyn Warren (https://sharynwarren.com/), Wise Woman Extraordinaire, to whom I have turned when the going got just tough enough.

~

# PART I

# INTRODUCTION TO THE JOURNEY

## *Lighting the Path*

Above the mountains
the geese turn into
the light again

Painting their
black silhouettes
on an open sky.

Sometimes everything
has to be
inscribed across
the heavens

so you can find
the one line
already written
inside you.

Sometimes it takes
a great sky
to find that

first, bright
and indescribable
wedge of freedom
in your own heart.

Sometimes with
the bones of the black
sticks left when the fire
has gone out

someone has written
something new
in the ashes of your life.

You are not leaving.
Even as the light fades quickly now,
you are arriving.

David Whyte, "The Journey," *House of Belonging*
Reprinted with permission

# CHAPTER ONE

~

# Considering Girls' Quests through the Lens of Hero and Heroine Journeys

Therapeutically mapping a person's symbolic journey in the sand shows us a person's life as a heroic journey, progressing through critical emotional and developmental stages by meeting the challenges and vicissitudes of their lives with integrity and courage.

The hero's journey into manhood has been well theorized and studied (Campbell, 2008; Clift & Clift, 1991). A man's journey is often one of engagement in battling the world to prove worthiness, strength, and empowerment. "Someone—it's been attributed to everyone from Dostoyevsky to John Gardner—once said there are only two possible stories: a man goes on a journey, or a stranger comes to town" (Metcalf, 2007). This can be the way heroic stories begin—with struggles, difficulties, tensions, and changes in circumstances. The very idea that people are pulled into the unexpected by an unknown factor, or that our very nature leads us to deep places, is fascinating—and crucial to our work as therapists. We work with clients who chose to journey to find their inner treasure: that of wisdom, strength, and self-confidence.

In actuality, does the hero's journey fit the form of the heroine's quest? A few professionals, all women, have delineated the woman's journey to maturity and adulthood as needing a distinctly separate framework (Murdock, 2013; Frankel, 2010; Engelsman, 1993) for women's heroic pathways. We don't as yet have a well-developed model of this quest for girls, particularly with regard to sandplay and play therapy. Therapist Mary Pipher theorized originally in 1994 that preadolescent girls "can be androgynous, having the ability to act adaptively in any situation regardless of gender role constraints. An androgynous person can comfort a baby or change a tire, cook a meal or chair a meeting. Research has shown that, since they are free to act without worrying if their behavior is feminine or masculine, androgynous adults are the most well adjusted" (Pipher, 2005, p.18).

The premise of this book, however, is that the girl's journey is generally quite distinct from that of a boy's journey, based upon cultural, genetic, gender, social, learning, and developmental factors. These factors often combine with constraints upon girls in today's culture to repress assertive energies, to hide intellectual strengths, and conform to some ideal of femininity (Simmons, 2010, 2011). A recent study by Breslau et al. (2017) utilized a large and nationally representative sample of children and adolescents between 12 and 17 years of age, examining sex differences in the incidence of first-onset depression (i.e., "defined by reports of first-in-lifetime depressive episode with onset within 1 year of age prior to interview, including suicide attempts during that episode"). The prevalence of recent first-onset depression was found to be sizably higher for girls than for boys at every age, reaching the highest incidence at age 15 for girls. Nearly three times as many girls (36.1%) as boys (13.6%) experienced their first onset of depression between the ages of 12 and 17. Many of the girls in the study reported first-onset of depressive episode as young as 11 years of age.

Girls in particular must mediate expectations from without and within. The need to self-regulate with regard to our emotional states and the situations in which girls find themselves, is crucial to living bravely, creatively, and well through the challenges, traumatic experiences, and obstacles encountered in daily life. Siegel (2015) and van der Kolk (2014) have written compelling material on this subject with particular regard to adults, based upon solid research. "When we attune to others we allow our own internal state to shift, to come to resonate with the inner world of another. This resonance is at the heart of the important sense of 'feeling felt' that emerges in close relationships. Children need attunement to feel secure and to develop well and . . . feel close and connected. . . . When we are in emotional balance, we feel alive and at ease. Our feelings are aroused enough for life to have meaning and vitality, but not so aroused that we feel overwhelmed or out of control. Lacking balance, we move toward either excessive arousal, a state of chaos, or too little arousal, a state of rigidity or depression. Either extreme drains us of vitality" (Siegel, p. 27).

Cyberbullying, aggression, and feminine idealization within the culture of elementary and middle-school girl groups demands that we as therapists assist girls to develop abilities to inhibit fear-based or aggressive impulses and modulate anxious responses within a social context in school and with social media (Wiseman, 2016; Simmons, 2011; Hains, 2014; Orenstein, 2012). Psychoeducational guidance and therapy that encourages "focused attunement with another person can shift us out of disorganized and fearful states" (van der Kolk, 2014, p. 78). Siegel and Bryson (2012) have written a book of strategies for children needing to manage more regulated, calm states in particular. Shih et al. (2006), as quoted in Green (2014, p. 45), reported that "Touching and playing in the sand may produce a calming effect on anxious or disruptive preschool children."

For our girls, dealing as they are with brutally crushing internal and external forces, what is needed is targeted therapeutic assistance to encourage positive self-attribution, and strengthen confidence and resourceful persistence. Whether we're working with girl bullying (Wiseman, 2016), overwhelming stress for girls at school and at home (Cohen-Sandler, 2005), or the myth of being the "good" and "perfect" girl (Simmons, 2010, 2011), clinically examining a journey of this magnitude warrants focused attention and flexibility as practitioners. Signell emphasizes that:

"Girls and women live in a world that is dominated by aggressive forces" (1990, p. 79), in which a "discerning heart" (p. 155) must prevail in order to reclaim agency for herself, and for the girl both academically and socially.

Why is this important? It depends on your training as well as your other racial, cultural, religious, and therapeutic perspectives, for example. Children experience powerful urges to change and push through "stuck" places in order to grow and develop. Despair, anger, and frustration can rip through hard-won resilience and leave feelings of emptiness behind when our clients become overwhelmed by traumatic experience, family disconnection, increasing cultural, social, relational, and academic pressures. As therapists, we don't want our clients—or ourselves, for that matter—to give up or burn out.

As a therapist, do you ascribe to more of an internal or external locus of control for yourself and for your clients? What are your political views, and how might they impact your client work? Which theoretical stance do you take as a therapist? How can we approach our work with clients with cultural humility, that is "the basic assumption that in each and every interaction, there is something that we do not know or understand" (Loue, 2012, p. 108)? Sandplay invites self-examination of beliefs and attitudes about the people with whom we come in contact throughout our professional (and personal) life. Over our lifespan, these beliefs, stances, and perspectives greatly influence the therapeutic process and can lead us to discover what is unique about individual client journeys.

There is more than a "nod" needed to express and address the complexity of gender, spiritual and multicultural and multiracial diversity in our children and in their homes. Parental and societal response to gender-variant, gender-fluid, or gender-nonconforming children proves crucial in positive identification in self-image and confidence (Brill & Pepper, 2008, p. xiv). Providing options to children about gender-fluid choices and perspectives is, of course, optimal. In terms of the scope of this book, we will use the "she" and "her" pronouns to encompass the experience of what is termed the "girl" or "girl's" experience, meaning the "feminine" aspect of gender experience in general terms. Estelle Weinrib, a Jungian analyst and sandplay therapist and founding member of the national sandplay organization in the United States, related in her book *Images of the Self* (2004, pp. 38–39):

> As used in this work, the term feminine is not limited to the female gender. The Jungian view is that all of us are to some extent androgynous. Just as we all have male and female hormones, so we carry contrasexual psychological characteristics; different modes of perceiving, thinking, acting, reacting and relating. For those who object to using the terms masculine and feminine, one could as easily use the Eastern Asian terms of Yang and Yin, or Logos and Eros, or A and B. . . . The feminine qualities in men are personified by the term anima. In women, the masculine counterpart is called the animus.

In other words, the use of the term *young feminine*, with regard to these modes and identities seems unnecessarily clinical; we will stick to the term *girl* for all intents and purposes.

## The Hero and Heroine Journey Maps

To journey, according to the online Merriam-Webster dictionary, can mean "something suggesting travel or passage from one place to another" (e.g., the journey from youth to maturity or a journey through time). Since the first human exhibited the courage to take care of their group, invent a tool, or begin to hunger for a change in the focus of their lives or in the lives of their community, there have been paths forged for the hero or heroine's journey.

Joseph Campbell first delineated the hero's journey in a visually oriented diagram (2008, pp. 245–46). He separated the journey into three parts: Departure, Initiation, and Return. He describes the adventure of the hero through encounters with shadow, and the "kingdom of the dark," illuminating the heroic journey through battles and meetings with magical beings.

> Beyond the threshold, then, the hero journeys through a world of unfamiliar yet strangely intimate forces, some of which severely threaten him (tests), some of which give magical aid (helpers). When he arrives at the nadir of the mythological round, he undergoes a supreme ordeal and gains his reward. The triumph may be represented as . . . an expansion of consciousness and therewith of being (illumination, transfiguration, freedom). The final work is that of the return. . . . The boon that he brings restores the world (elixir) (p. 246).

Campbell's representation of the hero's journey follows a circular map that goes in a counterclockwise fashion.

Clift and Clift (1988) expand the understanding of the hero's journey through dreamwork and active imagination by examining the heroic quest and the hero's growth in consciousness and purpose during the journey. They expand on the motifs of this journeying in dreams and through illustrating the symbols of transformation in the stages of the hero's journey.

The heroic quest for women was redefined by Murdock (2013). She presented an analysis of the adult woman's heroine's journey through nine stages of psychospiritual development for women. The journey entailed an initial separation from traditional feminine values, which sought recognition and success through a masculine-defined world lens; then the experience of spiritual aridity and the letting-go aspect of death with regard to traditional non-valuing of women; and a turn inward to reclaim the power and spirit of feminine nature. The final stages of this model involve an acknowledgement of the union and power of one's dual nature (both the masculine and the feminine aspects) for the benefit of all people (Murdock, 2013).

Her model accounts for aspects of separation, healing, and integration of masculine and feminine in the female psyche, as well as the loneliness and emptiness of many women in midlife, and the need to "reconnect" with the power inherent in a woman's body, mind, and spirit. She focuses on how daughters and mothers can come together in understanding so that wounding can be healed. Although Murdock makes use of Campbell's model (i.e., the Road of Trials, Finding the Boon of Success, Initiation and Descent to the Goddess), she enriches our awareness that there are other ways to examine a woman's path to individuation and meaning. Her model moves clockwise from the top in a circle.

Joan Engelsman's book (1993) offers an enlivening means of discerning a woman's inner wants and truths with regard to this journey as well. With rich imagery, she explores the idea of taking back what was given away to a host of relatives, partners, children, siblings, and friends/acquaintances. She examines the dynamics of focusing and caring for the self, and how to weave one's own "cloth of gold" from the return and reworking of those energies in the taking back of what needs to be re-owned. Curiously, women's parental influences are missing from this grand story.

Frankel's (2010) vision of the heroine's journey incorporates Campbell's quest cycle with nods to powerful forces such as shadow energy, the "Sacred Wedding" of the animus and anima within the woman's psyche, and mentorship. Frankel's stages of the woman's journey is explained through world stories, myth, and legends. These traverse from what she names "Innocence and Discovery," through the "Journey through the Unconscious," "Meeting the Other," "Meeting the Self," to "Goddesshood and Wholeness." The stories found from differing cultures illustrate the crossing of thresholds of the quest. Although Frankel's title speaks of girls, her stories primarily focus on the pathways for mature women. Her model runs counterclockwise and uses many of the thresholds, as Campbell's journey model does, within a storytelling format.

Ryce-Menuhin created what he termed *The First Mapping of Sandplay Forms*. This measurement pertained to the areas of the individual trays in which "maps of tendencies present in sandplayers' psyche" manifest (1992, p. 97). He noted:

> There has tended to be a tacit agreement among most of my sandplay colleagues not to "map" the areas of the sandtrays pertaining to areas of psyche being projected. This is a too easy refusal to discuss the difficulties of observing tendencies which occur over great numbers of sandplays. . . . There are three principal levels of psyche being projected into sandplay: the conscious level, the level of the personal unconscious and the level of the collective (archetypal) unconscious (p. 91).

Sandplay teacher Geri Grubbs devised a descriptive methodology to assess sandtrays for research and training called the Sandplay Categorical Checklist for Sandplay Analysis (2005).

In 1998 sandplay teaching member Betty Jackson worked with a group of therapists for sandplay consultation in Pennsylvania. She presented a visual model of the Sandplay Journey as a circle with four quarters and a threshold at each quarter (unpublished manuscript). She based her formulation in part on Joseph Campbell's perspective of the hero's journey. I found this model quite helpful in understanding client work in the sand. I referred to it in my case write-up for sandplay teacher certification requirements with the International Society of Sandplay Therapists (www.isst-society.com), which was later published in the *Journal of Sandplay Therapy* (Heiko, 2008). Jackson conceptualized a circular journey ("Into the Labyrinth: Exploring the Stages of Sandplay Process") with four parts plus a mid-journey centering. This included an initial problem statement, securing the "free and protected space," resistance and descent into the unconscious; confrontation with shadow and movement toward centering;

reconciling the tension of the opposites and an ascent from the unconscious and integration into daily life.

Jackson published a somewhat different model of the "Cyclical Stages of the Archetypal Journey." She emphasized Campbell's stages and likened the quarters of the journey to solstice and equinox times at the beginning, middle, and end of the year. She did not keep the four gateways from her earlier model, but in the first gateway added: "Answering the Call," "Commitment," and "Preparation" (Friedman & Mitchell, 1994, p. 55).

Since 2000 I have continued to refine this model in my work with clients and in teaching therapists about sandplay. When our clients make the heart's journey to wholeness through the sand, through story and play, they can begin to heal and even transform their suffering into meaningful perspectives. This helps build up resiliency and guides our clients into healthy ways of coping with feelings of despair, fear, and helplessness. Therapists can offer these children opportunities to process their struggles through sandplay and in better understanding the journey stages themselves.

# CHAPTER TWO

~

# The Clinical Background of Sandplay

## History and Process

Children's therapeutic work in the sand was originally conceived by Margaret Lowenfeld in London and expanded upon by Dora M. Kalff of Switzerland. Of Lowenfeld, Kalff said that "She understood how to place herself in the world of the child. With ingenious intuition she created a game that enables the child to build a world, his world, in a sand box" (Kalff, 2004, p.16). According to Martin Kalff, his mother was introduced to Lowenfeld's work at a conference in Zurich, near Kalff's home. He added that "My mother recognized the great value of this method and decided to study with Lowenfeld. . . . In 1956, she began her yearlong study. . . . While doing her work with the World Technique in England, and later in her practice in Zollikon, Switzerland, my mother recognized that the creations of the children in the sand correspond to the inner psychic processes of individuation described by C. G. Jung. She developed her own method for working with these patterns of individuation in the children's work and, in agreement with Margaret Lowenfeld, she called this method sandplay (Kalff, 2004, p. vii). Most recently, Lowenfeld's approach is the focus of Roxanne Rae's clinical case studies with a neurobiological lens (2015). According to the Colorado Sandplay Therapy Association's "Sandplay Influences" page,

> One summer the daughter of psychiatrist C. G. Jung vacationed nearby and noticed her own children appeared unusually content when they returned from play at Kalff's. Impressed with her gift of providing an environment soothing to children, Jung's daughter suggested to Kalff that she study psychology and introduced her to her father. Kalff took the challenge and during the course of her training, with Jung's encouragement, she spent a year in England (http://sandplaytherapy.org/?page_id=64).

Sandplay and sandtray methods have become popular throughout the United States and internationally since Kalff began presenting lectures in California to the

Jungian communities there from the 1960s until her death in 1990. Sandplay evolved through Kalff's combining and refining Carl Jung's work, her studies in London with her mentor Margaret Lowenfeld at the Institute of Child Psychology using "The World Technique," and Tibetan Buddhist principles. One of the Tibetan Buddhist Lamas lived with Frau Kalff when many monks emigrated to Switzerland after the government went into exile in 1959. Kalff met with the Dalai Lama several times during her lifetime and became a practitioner of Buddhist principles.

The three roots of sandplay therapy twine together to form the tree of sandplay's heritage. Tibetan Buddhist silent witnessing; Lowenfeld's use of sand, water, and miniatures; and Jung's perspective on wholeness and the spiritual growth of the psyche all contribute to an understanding of what illuminates a sandplay journey. It is the path to understanding what is valuable for each being. That may take the form of understanding "I am lovable," "I must get control of my temper," or it may be "the reason I am here is to nurture my self-awareness and confidence." For each person, each client, the task is set in sand: forming and re-forming as age, gender, spirit, knowledge, developmental stage, and so forth emerge.

Kalff spoke about the psychic development of her clients in sandplay by using one of the commentaries of the I Ching. She likened the flow of water to the therapeutic nature of the relationship of sand, symbol, client, and therapist in pursuit of healing goals:

> It . . . merely fills up all of the places through which it flows; it does not shrink from any dangerous spot nor from any plunge, and nothing can make it lose its own essential nature. It remains true to itself under all conditions. Thus likewise, if one is sincere when confronted with difficulties, the heart can penetrate the meaning of the situation. And once we have gained inner mastery of a problem, it will come about naturally that the action we take will succeed (2004, p. 115).

In sandplay, clients are presented with a rectangular shallow tray, the dimensions of which measure 28.5 x 19.5 x 3 inches, the size corresponding "exactly to what the eye can encompass" (Kalff, 2004, p.16). The trays are coated with blue marine-grade paint so that the tray is waterproofed and the color is similar to that of the sky or of the water. The tray is halfway filled with sand and the room in which the clients work contain a selection of differently sized miniatures. These symbols may represent anything and everything found in the world (i.e., houses, animals, cars, traffic signs, people, fantasy figures, archetypal symbols). The collection of miniatures is actually a reflection of the clinician's culture, worldview, and personal symbolic representations. Clients are usually presented with a choice of two trays: one that is waterproofed and with which the client can wet to whatever degree she or he and the clinician are comfortable; and one that remains dry.

Why might a therapist offer sandtrays with availability to sprinkle, pour, or thoroughly wet with water? Sandtrays that invite actual, not just symbolically represented, water (such as ponds, felt "lakes," plastic or resin waterfalls, plastic ice floes) to be used throughout or in client-designated portions allow clients to experience a deep connection to the unconscious aspect of being. Pouring, trickling, sprinkling, spraying and creating channels, inlets, rivers, and the flow of actual water can welcome a satisfying involvement with the emotional realm of the senses and experience. Dry sand can give a sense of this connection and experience, but only to a certain depth, since it can't be molded or shaped without water. Traditional use of play sand or specialty sand sources incorporates sand that has been cleaned and is generally free of dust. I use microbead sand from a construction supplier and specialty sands from a geologist; I find that children enjoy the quality of authentic sand rather than kinetic sand.

I also make several other trays available throughout my playroom in terms of garnet stone sand and tubs that the clients can fill with water (called "flooded trays") or mix sand in with the water to whatever level they desire. I deliberately did not include a sink in the playroom in my office, but keep a large container of water handy. This way, the client and I walk to the business office or the bathroom nearby to fill up water containers, or I will get the water for the client, thereby adding some deliberation and control to the process of choosing water-related activities. My office is accessible only to myself and an office partner, assuring sheltered and contained trips to get more water if more is needed.

The sandplay process invites the client to choose from among the miniatures to make a picture in the sand, representing their world, their issues, their feelings, or possibly a dream. The therapist provides a "safe and protected space" for the client to play out their issues, conflicts, and nature in the relational space afforded through the tray between therapist and client. According to Kalff, the clinician provides this space by accepting the client fully, working to appreciate the client's emotional states and conflicts as represented in the trays. "Feeling sheltered is a prerequisite for all true freedom and for the freedom to develop," Kalff maintained (2004, p. 115). I prefer using the word "sheltered," as it encompasses both protection and harboring refuge for our child clients. I suggest to all clients that they see what their hands want to do. Children don't need more instruction than that, I find, especially when the parents and therapist have spent time in a previous session discussing expectations for the family and child in therapy, and outlining specific emotional and behavioral goals for the child and parents.

The sandtray is left intact when the client leaves the session. The therapist then takes slides of the sandtray in order to assist in diagnosis, treatment planning, and general tracking of the therapeutic progress of the client. Supervision and continued training in sandplay interpretation is vital to this process of understanding the client's use, placement, and personal meaning regarding the symbolic miniatures in the sandtray.

Often the first tray lays out the problem or problems the client is experiencing (Kalff, 2004, p. 9) as well as the resources needed to address them. First sandtrays, especially those of young children, are typically more chaotic, including themes of strong conflict. Other themes emerge and evolve over the course of treatment as the client works though various issues. The sandplay journey process is a spiral journey, encompassing a "slice of life" in the great round of that person's experience and lifetime. When the self emerges through centering (i.e., in trays that symbolically represent the "constellation of the self," where the self symbolically meets the psyche in relation to transcendent or "bridging" energies), more peaceful and numinous representations emerge. During this process the client confronts and integrates her shadow material and the tension of opposite needs, emotions, and experiences and begins to integrate that perspective and manifest more harmonious energies.

The process of creating the sandtray enables the client to express both conscious and unconscious material. Emotions and difficulties can be worked through and various aspects of these conflicts or personality issues can be integrated. The result can help bring clients to a state of "wholeness"—always, of course, with the proviso that continued processing and awareness of emotional material can bring deeper and more meaningful spiritual understanding of that client's psyche at the different stages and challenges of life.

Frau Dora Kalff initially taught the sandplay method using the oral tradition. She described her clinical work by presenting 35mm slides of sandplay trays in lectures. This tradition of interpreting the sandplay process was enlarged and delineated by many of her adherents using a descriptive verbal and written format. Sandplay practitioners have come a long way and currently use digital slides for case presentations.

Only Kalffian work in the sand is referred to as sandplay (i.e., *sandspiel* in the original Swiss-German). All other therapies using sand are referred to as sandtray work or sand therapy (see Rae, 2015; or Homeyer, 2010). Kalffian sandplay is also distinguished by a strong emphasis on personal process of the therapist in the sand. Sandplay therapy, then, is experienced first by the clinician who engages with his or her own sandplay therapist in as complete a way as possible—and only after that with clients. My role with clients is metaphorically that of a river guide. I have done my work to navigate the metaphorical river of the psyche (realizing I am never "finished" with learning it): its present and past course, its currents, its temperature—and now can take the journey on it with others, those who ride the waves in their own boats.

Thus the therapist completes an arc of her own journey, in whatever stage of life in which she finds herself. Each therapist choosing this path will begin to meet vulnerability and personal challenges with as much of their personal resources and bravery as she can muster. The therapist stands in front of wet and dry sandtrays and begins the journey through sand in her own "process," completing that round of the life journey. The clinician can then be certified by the International Society of Sandplay Therapists (ISST), along with meeting other standardized criteria) to then adopt sandplay with clients. There are ISST component societies all over the world (in the United States, there is the Sandplay Therapists of America).

As with many therapeutic modalities, sandplay offers a means of conveying the client's experience through a narrative. "Stories are complex. . . . In the play *Coming from a Great Distance*, by the Traveling Jewish Theater, it is said that 'Stories go in circles. They don't go in straight lines.' And so it is. And also '. . . there are stories inside stories and stories between stories and finding your way through them is as easy and as hard as finding your way home.' . . . We are called . . . to 'listen in circles', so we can find our way through them, can find our way home" (Simmons, 2011, p. x).

Certainly not every therapeutic or individual journey completes a full cycle. There are times when children leave therapy as a result of financial considerations, the ability to work comfortably with the therapist or with sand for sensory reasons, or in terms of their interest level. Joanna Bull spoke about Gilda Radner: "Gilda's book ends with her acceptance of what I had called, in working with her, 'delicious ambiguity,' the freedom that comes with simply not knowing the outcome of every happening or happenstance. For some, it is playful and curious and just exciting to go down a path that has so much potential" (1989, p. 260–261). The child who stares down into the sandtray and finds herself overwhelmed with anxiety may need reassurance that this modality may just not be an avenue for exploration at that time. With these children, I suggest other play therapy methods and a chance to work in the sand if and when they are ready.

Dora Kalff said that "We may encounter interruptions in treatment. It is often very difficult for the parents of troubled children to have the necessary understanding and patience to wait for a complete cure. This is particularly true because we are dealing with the irrational events of a hidden psychic process. Additionally, when signs of improvement become evident in the children after a short time, it can be especially difficult for the parents to understand the need to remain in treatment a while longer" (2004, p. 139). Although today we wouldn't speak of a "cure," we can use anticipatory guidance to help parents understand the needs of their children to continue their sandplay work until most of a journey cycle is completed.

## Essential Features of Sandplay Practice

Since the therapist experiences the sandplay journey themselves in the "process," it is left up to the therapist whether they feel they can contain the energy and focus of more than one client in a session. Certainly, considerations of space, finances, logistics, and relationship all play a part in determining whether a sandplay therapist will work with partners, a couple, siblings, or lead a demonstration of sandplay practice by having small groups or two therapists practice holding space and working together on a task involving symbols in the sand. Fundamentally, in sandplay the client is the one who decides to touch the sand or place symbols in a tray. The tray becomes an extension of self, of the psyche's expression of embodied emotion and thought. This aspect hugely affects family work, parent-child work, and the therapeutic relationship. If the client is more than one person during a session—a couple, a family, siblings—therapists can create (and assist in maintaining) clear boundaries around moving someone else's figures, verbalizing praise or having participants ask questions.

One of the most difficult and actually one of the most sophisticated requirements of sandplay is that the therapist holds their reactions to tray creation (i.e., leaving off saying "wow, that's beautiful" or "you must be feeling scared right now"). Keeping the tenet of mindful witnessing foremost in the practice of sandplay is vital. Sandplay therapists try to be mindful and think about the purpose of making a particular comment or interpretation before speaking over the tray. When a client asks for a reaction, hesitating and breathing deeply is essential as a first response. Then, if it seems necessary, the therapist can give a response. The client trusts us to honor their psyche and not intrude on their process or their need to struggle a bit in order to work through a particular difficulty.

Trusting the relational field between therapist and client, that connection of safety and active listening and holding is central to sandplay. It's not essential for us as therapists to understand everything that's happening in the tray at the time of the client's creation, or make verbal links to the client between the symbol material and what's happening in the client's everyday life (the process called *interpretation*). Through years of practice, I find myself letting go of the need to understand what's happening at the cognitive level at any given time in a session. I try to remember that the struggle to understand during the client session may interfere with learning about the client's experience of their story and their emotions during a session. It's all a process of "a mutual coming to understand," as Bradway and McCoard (1997, p. 28) pointed out when reviewing her own trays ten years after completing her process with Dora Kalff.

Here are the main suggestions I make to those I supervise and consult in sandplay practice when watching tray creation:

1. *Just take it all in.* The child usually has spent all or most of the session creating their tray, often within the context of an overall play therapy experience. There has been a whirlwind of verbalizations, noises of dropped miniatures or humming, a swirl of colors, shapes, and movement over the 45 minutes of the session. Complex themes have been interwoven through the tray creation by the child's psyche. That is so grand, so important, and so intense—even if at first the tray seems very simple in construction.

2. *Remember to breathe deeply and fully.* When we concentrate too intensely, trying to "get it right," we often forget something as simple as literally taking a breath and not holding it. Allowing ourselves to breathe deeply and let that flow of dynamic tension ease comfortably through our body allows us to truly experience what is happening in the moment, in the co-transference with our client.

3. *Hold the space.* We need to listen closely to the client. Our attention wanders, and we bring it back to the present moment in a mindful manner so that we may meet the client's unspoken, unconscious material, as well as the consciously recognized verbalizations or demands, in a compassionate manner. Often it is what is missing in the tray—the elements, the symbols, what the client could say but doesn't—that is the place of the client's vulnerability and crucial to understanding the client's unconscious process. We can find that place more easily if we quiet our mind and stay focused on the present moment.

4. *Try to be patient.* Notice the nonverbal, verbal, sensory, mood, affect, story development (if any), energy, and activity level of your client and her creation in the tray. Keep the breath going steadily and comfortably while noticing these dynamics and aspects of presentation. Ryce-Menuhin held that the act of silently looking at the tray, and then intently sharing without words the client's creation, "can enable the (client) to reveal aspects and subtleties of thought and feeling, intuition and sensation which both their speech and gesture may

fail to present. The non-verbal feedback of just looking and intensely sharing the (client's) sandplay has, in itself, a great power to clarify the situation for the therapist" (1992, p. 4).

5. *Hold your comments and your interpretations for consultation time.* Being present means that we are actively engaged in experiencing what our client wants to express. Try not to make any suggestions to the client about what feelings or motive they may be experiencing or give them any homework assignments about what they might want to learn more about—in effect, to *try not to discuss anything directly over the tray.* We need to think seriously about whether we really want to make a particular comment and begin to thoroughly examine our own responses before sharing them with the client. When the client asks for our preferences or reaction, we need to first breathe—and then give a response that honors their psyche and does not intrude on their process. We need to ask ourselves: "Can I wait to talk this through in supervision or consultation so I'm not inserting my own projections and issues into the client's experience?"

6. *Try not to make any suggestions to the client about what feelings or motive they may be experiencing.* Many play therapists are trained to reflect emotions and track the client's process verbally in order to demonstrate attunement and enhance the transference. Psychoeducational training about different emotional or behavioral topics, cognitive-behavioral therapy, or directive play therapy often plays a vital role in our work with children. It's just not the right time to insert those strategies into the sandplay process, unless the therapist is using directed sandtray strategies for a specific purpose. The experience of sandtray demands that we be present to and with the client in a more nonverbally attuned way, through our shared sense of humor and the conveyance of companionship through our warmth and presence.

7. *Allow the client to be in a heightened state of "not knowing."* This is what Pearson and Wilson (2001) mean when they suggest tolerating a sense of the client's "creative doubt." After seeing that a tray is finished, the therapist might say, "Let's spend a few moments looking at the tray together." Asking the client, "Does this place (or tray) have a name?" or "Is there a story you'd like to share?" are good ways to elicit relevant client responses. The therapist might then suggest that both therapist and client move to another area, away from standing or sitting near the tray to talk about any associations or spontaneous responses the client generates. Sandplay therapists avoid directive, leading questions, or statements (i.e., "Is that wicked witch like your mother?" or "That elephant in the corner looks lonely."). The nature of sandplay is to let things percolate on their own time in the client's unconscious, to be brought to consciousness by the client when she is ready for the natural processing to unfold. This allows time and space for personal material to emerge.

8. *Trust the relational field between you and the client,* that connection of safety and active listening/holding. It's not essential for us as therapists to understand everything that's happening in the tray at the time of the client's making it,

or make verbal links to the client between the symbolic material and what's happening in the client's everyday life (a process we call *interpretation*). Practice letting go of needing to understand what's happening at the cognitive level and remember that the struggle to understand during the client session may interfere with learning about the client's experience of their story and their emotions during the session. It's all a process of *coming to understand*, as Kalff put it.

9. *Don't assume that anybody already knows the meaning of a chosen symbol.* Many well-meaning sandplay and sandtray teachers tell trainees precisely what a symbol means. How can anyone be sure about what is found and represented in an individual's psyche at any given point in time, even if there is ample verbalization by the client? A symbol represents 360° of the possible meanings of whatever you think it is, encompassing the dark and light aspects of whether the symbol can be seen as positive, negative, or neutral. A thorough engagement with myth, legend, story, and history—as well as an understanding of the literal and metaphorical essence of the material embodiment of a symbol—is necessary for interpretation. Even then, sandplay therapists begin an interpretation cautiously, questioning aloud by beginning to analyze a symbol by saying, "I wonder" rather than "This symbol is . . ." Lowenfeld herself stated that

> a world-maker standing in front of an open drawer containing a number of representations of houses of different shapes and sizes took up a medium sized house and put it in the flat sand in the world tray. . . . To the individual who has taken up the house it may represent a house but it may also and with equal possibility represent nothing of the sort. It may be the nearest object he can find to stand for the idea of safety, of being under observation, of the restrictions of urban life, of family, or simply a conveniently sized and shaped rectangular object she can use as a plinth later to put a horseman on to form a statue (1979, p. 255).

## Sandplay Practice within the Context of Integrative Child Therapies and Non-Directive Approaches

In their book *Integrative Play Therapy*, Drewes, Bratton, and Schaefer (2011) reflect on the history, efficacy, and practicality of blending diverse therapies in child clinical practice. This approach can build on the successes and strengths of diverse therapist backgrounds and skills, as well as modalities available to relieve the suffering of child clients and offer healing strategies. Olson-Morrison states that "An integrative model of play therapy combines empirically supported, evidenced-based, directive methods in trauma treatment with developmentally appropriate, insight-oriented, and nondirective models of play therapy . . . (which allows) the therapist to have flexibility in methods of treatment" (2017, p. 176). Using this model, typically therapists focus on the client's treatment with nondirective strategies first, and subsequently adopt directive, cognitive-behavioral intervention when needed in phase-based treatment of trauma (Green & Myrick, 2014; Gil, 2009).

A number of recent studies have referenced using sandtrays and sandplay as one of the myriad successful techniques in play therapy treatment (Green & Myrick, 2014; Green, Myrick & Crenshaw, 2013), along with other expressive modalities such as mandala-making, art, dance, and music. In my own practice, expressive art modalities, music, bibliotherapy, EMDR, clinical hypnosis, guided imagery, family and filial therapy methods are all utilized as part of comprehensive and integrative work in my offices with children, alongside the sandplay focus, which most children choose.

In the past, it has been stated that sandplay is seen as a "nonverbal" therapeutic method (Weinrib, 2004, p.1), most recently, by Eliana Gil, a founder of the play therapy movement in the United States (personal communication, May 27, 2017). Gil states ". . . most people associate sandplay with nonverbal, noninterpretive type of work." However, many adult and child clients do verbalize while creating trays. They weave stories into the processing of tray creation or spontaneously speak seemingly of unrelated events. Many clients analyze their own process of making the trays through a "meta-analysis" of what some of the figures and symbols they chose might mean to them. Therapists ask the client if they need a figure, or would like some help at times, and may engage with the client during the tray-making with facial and other gestures, as well as in reassuring speech. At the completion of a tray, the sandplay therapist may ask, "Do you have a name for this tray?" and sometimes, "Is there a story about this tray you'd like to share?"

Kalff, sandplay's founder, described the play of one of her child clients as "not what I was striving for in that moment. So I intervened to guide him for the first time in the therapy" (2004, p. 47). Kalff understood that when strong shadow aspects were played out fully, there is a crucial moment for client and therapist in therapy. "It is not often easy to recognize this turning point, but it is one of the most important moments in therapy. If the therapist misses it, there is danger that energies which had been set free will become permanently destructive. For this reason it is extremely important the newly awakened energies are caught by the therapist and led into constructive paths" (p. 47). In one situation, Kalff helped a boy use a blowtorch constructively to remove old paint from beams, instead of dripping the fuel in the blowtorch onto the ground. "Now this was interesting! The enthusiasm for this game, which had turned into work, lasted for hours. The same energies that dissolved the paint with the flame instantly took a positive effect as the beautiful old wood of the beams reappeared" (p.48).

In sandplay there is no directed analysis of meaning of any of the conscious or unconscious material or symbols over the tray before, during, or after the client finishes sandwork. Of course, verbal interpretation through client and therapist interaction and "talk therapy" may commonly occur—*just not over the tray*. As Weinrib states,

> The aim of sandplay is to offer really free play, devoid of rules and in safe circumstances. It offers an opportunity for being and doing without encumbrances. To press for associations would be to encourage cerebral activity, which is not desirable here except in its most spontaneous exercise. . . . The therapist is, of course, free to use any ideas he or she has derived from the sandplay process in an indirect way in the verbal analysis. In fact,

the patient's response to the introduction of these ideas provides one way to check on the validity of the analyst's "reading" of the pictures (2004, p. 13).

Thus sandplay engages the client through the relationship with the therapist in a sometimes nonverbally active and sometimes quite verbally active way, although not by directing client movements or analyzing sandtray dynamics with clients while the client is engaged in creating the tray.

Pattis Zoja's analysis of sandplay emphasizes that

> it deals with preverbal and pre symbolic areas of experience by way of the shaping and manipulation of concrete objects. The hands assume the leading role: the body assumes the leading role. Not narrative not language. Sandplay follows the patient into his or her particular phase of development, and its flexibility is sufficiently great as to allow it completely to adapt itself to whatever the patient's current needs (2004, p. 19).

## The Container of the Co-Transference in the Relational Field

Sandplay Therapists of America founding member Kay Bradway coined the term *co-transference* to refer to this nonhierarchical relationship between client and therapist. She spoke of using the term

> to designate the therapeutic feeling relationship between therapist and patient. These inter-feelings seem to take place almost simultaneously, rather than sequentially as the composite term transference-countertransference suggests. These feelings are, I believe, necessarily determined by both earlier and current happenings. And it is not just the person coming for therapy who projects; the therapist does also. Both may find hooks in the other on which to hang, or project, the unused or repressed parts of themselves, or personal memories from the past, or archetypal images. And both respond to these projections. . . . Moreover, both projections and responses are often entirely at an unconscious level. The therapeutic relationship is a mix, a complex mix, a valuable mix. It is this mix that I am referring to when I use the term co-transference (1992, p. 33).

A Kalffian sandplay therapist accompanies the client by providing their presence, their mindful attention to the client with flexibility and ease wherein the resonance between therapist and client further engages depth and breadth to the work. The co-transference can be viewed as an encompassing and evolving concept, whereby the psyche of therapist and client relationally has an impact on the other (Cunningham, 2013, p. 67).

There is an inherent wisdom in the core belief that human beings come to a state of wholeness and integration when given the freedom, space, and respectful regard in the therapeutic container of sandplay. Sandplay teacher and founding member Hayao Kawai said, "Learn to do nothing. Well." This seemingly simple statement took on the nature of a koan for me over the years. I found more and more challenges in its meaning.

> New and seasoned counselors alike can benefit from reminding themselves that our presence with families means, simply, the state of being present to and with them.

Counselors do this by sharing time, energy, creativity, focus, teachings and knowledge, giving each family the fullest and most imperfectly complete attention possible. Family counselors share enthusiasm, questions, heartfelt concern, confusion, and apologies for making mistakes, failing to understand, or neglecting to respect what has been presented in sessions. It doesn't mean silence, although at times silence is required of therapists (Heiko, 2015, p.186).

The term *temenos*, in Kalffian therapy, thus relates to the holding environment, the "container," whereby the therapist creates a predictable, nonjudgmental, and safe environment that allows the client space to freely express herself in sandplay and in verbal and nonverbal interactions with the therapist. The therapist creates safety by protecting the person's privacy, honoring their uniqueness, and at the same time defining the limits of the "holding" space (Kalff, 2004; Bradway & McCoard, 1997; Cunningham, 2013; Weinrib, 2004). According to Cunningham, "It is through the relational container that symbols are understood and the Self is constellated." (p. 1). The therapist must be prepared to accept the person's shadow material, allowing for its identification, integration, and incorporation into the psyche of the client, as well as be prepared to own her shadow material as well. Experienced and beginning therapists make a commitment to maintain a questioning and humble stance regarding their own journeys, through finding their own therapist and participating in group and/or individual consultation and supervision activities.

Play therapists naturally use strategies that include symbol play and metaphors. Interpreting each symbol leads us to understand that it is more than just one thing, a perspective that includes many layers of meaning and association. We need to use the trait of perseverance to continue to flex our cognitive and emotional flexibility in situations involving families and with our own reactions to family play sessions. Elkhart Tolle expressed this comprehensive perspective by affirming, "I cannot tell you any spiritual truth that deep within you don't know already. All I can do is remind you of what you have forgotten" (2010, p. 6).

The therapist can provide a strong, reliable, mature adult presence as mentor, guide, and wise elder being for the child. As Green (2014, p. 35) notes: "Throughout psychotherapy, the play therapist absorbs and contains children's inner longings and desires, pain and sadness, murderous fantasies and destructive impulses, jealousy and tumultuous rage, and inner strength and resiliency."

Out of the thousands of very courageous girls I've worked with over 35 years, two girls gifted me with poems concerning what the work that we did together meant to each of them. One, "The Rose," was published in the *Journal of Sandplay Therapy* (Heiko, 2008). Another poem elucidates the quality of authentic engagement in the co-transference relationship. The client states, "But she is not a fairy godmother," and speaks to the tremendous effort this client needed to exercise with shadow energies. She continues: "She is the tallest tree in the misty woods helping you to see clearly through the fog, providing tart plums and cool shade through harsh days and lonely nights. . . . She is the shelter when storms surround the sky."

## Kalff's Sandplay Journey Model and Current Interpretation of Archetypal Themes

Initially Kalff taught and wrote about Neumann's work in tandem with the stages of sandplay. According to Mitchell and Friedman, she viewed these three stages as wounding, fighting, and adaptation to the collective (2015, p. 7). "In the first phase," Kalff stressed, "the ego expresses itself chiefly in pictures where animals and vegetation predominate. The next stage brings battles that appear again and again, especially during puberty. By now, the child is so strengthened that he can take upon himself the battle with external influences and is able to come to grips with them. Finally, he is admitted to the environment as a person and becomes a member of the collective" (2004, pp. 9–10).

Mitchell and Friedman (2017) recognized repeated patterns of specific archetypal themes in their work analyzing sandplay processes. They began tracking these themes to follow client progress in therapy. Two different themes emerged: wounding and healing, the former most often in the beginning phase of therapy and the latter at the ending phase of therapy. The wounding themes contained elements that were chaotic, empty/barren, split/barricaded, confined, neglected, hidden, prone, injured, threatened, or hindered. The healing themes were comprised of bridging, journeying, energized, going deeper, birthing, nurturing, changed, spiritual elements, centered and integrated elements of tray construction.

# CHAPTER THREE

~

# A Successful Sandplay Journey for a Girl from a Parent's Point of View

## Transcript

The best practice of integrative play therapy methods, and sandplay in particular, may prove frustrating for the parents to understand at first in treatment. An excellent article written by three sandplay teaching members (Kaplan, Punnett & Zappacosta, 2009) who collaborated on their approach to working with parents and families, details how the relationship with parents can be fostered using case examples.

The following is a transcript of a conversation between myself and the parent of one of the children with whom I worked (permission was granted by the parent to use this transcript). The conversation was unscripted: I had no idea what this parent might say, but chose to find out what her perspective on the therapy process was, in the larger context of a DVD project on introducing sandplay methods to clinicians. This parent's viewpoint elucidates important relational aspects of the sandplay journey. The parent talked about what she believed her daughter needed most: "to be able to learn to express herself in constructive ways." The mother believed that her daughter was in a self-destructive spiral. She was able to explain a number of key factors in the therapeutic treatment: the role of the unconscious in the psyche; the setup of the play therapy room itself; and her perspective on the first meeting of the child and therapist, with the parent present. This mother clearly understood that her child initially didn't want to express herself directly to anyone. Over time, as the therapeutic relationship developed, the mother realized that her daughter could eventually learn to feel safe when naming and examining her emotional responses.

RH: Tell us a little bit about your daughter . . .

Parent: My daughter is turning six next week, and she is full of life and energy. She is extremely dramatic, from the saddest of sad to the happiest of happiest; she is just incredibly dramatic and full of life.

RH: And when you brought her into my office, what were you looking for? What did you want from me?

Parent: I needed her to be able to learn to express herself in constructive ways. And I wanted her to be able to say when she was happy and when she was sad and when she was insecure or uncertain of something.

RH: It's brave to be able to say to somebody else, "The things I've been doing are not working in the way that I would like them to be working for my child. So could you help me to be able to do that?"

Parent: It's necessary because, if not, my daughter would have been in a pattern of self-destruction. If I didn't stop it at this point, it would just spiral out of control and it would have been harder to undo. So to me it was just an urgent need rather than an act of courage. It was like she was not going to work out well if we didn't stop it now.

RH: So you step in and do what needs to be done. And it's not a sure proposition and there's a lot of uncertainty and there needs to be some, I don't know what you'd call it, faith, trust, in trying this way.

Parent: I knew that trying an alternate method where she wasn't being put on the spot directly in questions and having to talk, she could just play and be observed and be understood. I just feel like the unconscious is a really powerful tool to understanding and unlocking whatever is troubling us. And when you explained how the sand tables represent the unconscious, it just made sense that this is the therapy that I thought could work for my daughter.

I remember you explaining it to me in the other room, how the therapy would work, how there were multiple sand tables and how she could pick out any toys that she wanted. And then when we came into the room, I saw the tables and I remember feeling very overwhelmed by all the choices of toys that she could play with. I felt like she would feel comfortable because things were on her level, like physically, the toys were on her eyesight level. The space was good for a child because they wouldn't feel too overwhelmed, they would be focused and channeled into playing and to stay on task and focused with the sand and with all the toys around. And so I just felt reassured by seeing the room and seeing all the options in the sand. I didn't understand why there were five or six sand tables! To me sand was sand, but obviously they're different . . . I mean there was brown sand and sand with different textures, so that's important for different kids who have different needs, you know?

I don't think she realized that she was actively communicating her feelings and her fears and what she likes and what she doesn't like through the kind of play that she did with you. And so she felt safer and probably much more open than she would have in another type of therapy environment.

RH: What struck me so much about meeting with you and talking with you was that you are a gifted person when it comes to the heart and your children's hearts, and also in terms of helping them express what's inside of them through art, through crafts. And that your daughter came in with this ability to be very comfortable with expressing herself actually that sometimes other children don't have.

Parent: Well, that's good because sometimes it takes her time to express herself with most people. It'll take several meetings, even with family members or neighbors or friends of mine. So for her to be able to walk into a new setting, she must have felt really reassured and comfortable with the environment. She's familiar with sand, most kids have played in the sandbox and she's familiar with knickknacks and toys, and you're a reassuring person, so she must have felt comfortable, you know, doing this. We talked about coming here to discuss her feelings. I don't think she realized that she was actively communicating her feelings and her fears and what she likes and what she doesn't like through the kind of play that she did with you. And so she felt safer and probably much more open than she would have in another type of therapy environment.

RH: Do you remember anything about when we first met in here with her?

Parent: I remember we came in and my daughter sat, I think, on that stool and she wouldn't look at you. She just sat to the side, and you kept talking to her even though she wouldn't look at you. And you told her stories about your own kids to try and make her feel more comfortable. Told her stories about your mom to make her feel more comfortable, and she still didn't want to buy into any of this. I think you talked to me about what I wanted for her, and she didn't really want to talk to me. And then I remember you letting her play. And I think she took out that cage and she took some lions, or I think a big lion, and put it in the cage and said, "There, it's locked up! Nothing's gonna get in and nothing's gonna get out!" And then I thought, we're gonna be in here for a long time. And so I remember, to me, that represented her feelings and saying, "Hey, you're not getting a part of this and I'm not giving you any either." And that was exactly why I came here because she was so guarded at home with what she would tell me about her fears, and so I was glad she did that because it really showed the essence of the problem. And I think she took some fairies or something, and they weren't going to get that lion out, that was just staying in there . . . he wasn't going to deal with anything. So I remember that very well.

I recall that you talked to my daughter and told her that you liked meeting with her and playing with her, and totally put the ball in her court and said, "If you want to come back and play, you can come back and play." And in my mind, we were coming back, but it gave her that sense of empowerment, to decide, to say, "Yes, I want to come back." Which is important to work through her problems in therapy or to say no and come back kicking and screaming. And I recall that we got into the car, and I said, "Do you want to go back and play with Miss Roz?" And she said, "Yes! I want to go back." So I said, "Okay, then we'll go back."

RH: Can you tell us anything about how you saw this unfolding from your point of view from her?

Parent: She never really talked much about what you guys did back here. I felt like I shouldn't really ask either because I felt like this was going to be . . . on her terms, this needed to be on her terms. And so I felt like she's going to share with me when she's ready. I remember one day when we came here, she was upset about your whiteboard not being sufficiently clean for her needs, and so she brought her own whiteboard cleaner and her own eraser, I think, and a pointer. I guess she wasn't happy with what you had [laughs]. To me that was a step to her feeling more comfortable, and that was so important to me because that showed me that she was comfortable to feel independent and to say, "This is what I need. I need to have this whiteboard clean and I'm going to take care of this myself. I'm going to take responsibility for it." And that was one of the things I wanted her to obtain out of therapy and to see her do that with you, who was not a stranger but not someone she sees every day. That was important for me to see her take that step. I saw that unfold through her.

She would be sad at times and I would ask her if she wanted to talk about it and she would say no. But then within five minutes, she would start to be able to give me some clues as to what she was upset about. So she would eventually start to talk and kind of let me in to see what was happening, to open up a dialogue. That felt good to see that. She was having anxiety with school that would show up physically, like she would have to use the bathroom frequently. That started to subside after, you know, a month or so of therapy. She wasn't using the bathroom frequently at school; she wasn't doing things that indicated stress while she was at school.

RH: I felt then that trust that you gave to me and that parents give, in the sense that when the child basically says, "This is my space, and Mom, Dad, could you be in the waiting room?" And then I give some indication [to the parents] of what's going on, but not a whole lot.

Parent: Well I felt like I would see in time some progress that was being made in my daughter and if I didn't see that progress, then I would have talked to you, and said, "What's going on? What are you guys working on? Because I don't think this is working for her at this point, or is this just going to take longer than I expected?" In fact, it happened much faster than I had expected; I thought that we would be on the six-month plan to be able to get her to where she is.

RH: I had said to you that sometimes this takes six to eight months.

Parent: Yeah, I just came in thinking before we even met that this was going to take a good six months, possibly a year, to help her establish herself better.

RH: You allowed her to get what she needed without pressuring in anyway. Because there are lots of financial and emotional kinds of constraints on people. You and I have talked a little bit about some of the stresses that people have in their lives and how in our different businesses sometimes we notice how irritated or irritable or how hard a time people have sometimes. How frightened people can be.

Parent: I think I just realized that for my daughter this is critical because, you know, I'm an adult and obviously I've been through things where I realize that if we don't allow her to express her feelings independently without judgment then she's just going to have that harder of a time as she grows older. And at least with me and with our family, that's critical for my kids to be able to say what they want, when they want, and how they want it within the realm of being respectful. But they have to be able to that with us. That's just priority and, to me, I would work a second job to be able to pay to make them do that, because that's the foundation for them to be able to deal with the rest of the world, to be able to stand up for themselves and to take a stance.

RH: What do you believe that your daughter learned from this experience of working in sand?

Parent: Her initial reaction when she feels uncertain or scared or anxious is to shut down, and she still does that right away. But she doesn't shut down for very long. And so I think in some sense, she has realized that she can express herself in some way to us.

Usually she does it through talk, direct talk. I have also found that she's been able to express herself with more opinions about things that may not necessarily be accurate, but at least those inner dialogues are coming out so we can help her see things in a different way. And so I think she's learned that it's safe to verbalize what's going on inside because she's got a lot going on inside. Because she told me for Halloween, she didn't know what to be because there were so many of her and she didn't know which one of her to pick because there's a lot of her inside, she told me. And you know, that's true.

And so I just know that . . . I know that this isn't going to last forever, that there's going to be more stresses that come into her life, that she's not going to know what to deal with. And so I just know that she'll be comfortable revisiting and coming back and learning to deal with things when we can't support her at home and she doesn't want us to be involved with whatever's bothering her. So at this point, I don't really have any questions because I just feel like everything was handled along the way and so I felt like, you know, I felt pretty confident and pretty secure with all that's happened.

*[I messed up on an appointment time for the interpretive with this mom, early in the therapy process, after about a month's time working with the child. Here is the last part of the transcript. I wasn't sure I would ask this question when I first started the interview. But it contained some valuable insights about the power of the sandplay process.]*

RH: I had made an appointment to do an interpretive with you for feedback. And I really messed up the appointment. Do you remember that?

Parent: Oh yeah.

RH: Oh yeah. And I tried to apologize and to fix that in some way, and you gave me another chance. Is it okay to ask if you would talk about that?

Parent: Yeah, that's fine. I don't usually give second chances. Ever.

RH: I got that sense from you.

Parent: Ever. I just, I don't anymore. I have given people second chances and it never really works out. But I felt like . . . I felt intuitively like this was what my daughter needed and I felt as though we started, and I felt as though she was comfortable and I had to step back and give this second chance as much as I didn't want to. And so I did, and I tried, and you know, I'm glad that I did because it all worked out in the end. So maybe I learned that sometimes people do need a second chance? I don't know. That might be pushing it [laughs]. But intuitively I just felt like this was appropriate for her and so I tried again.

RH: I'm very grateful to you for that and you said something before, you know, that sometimes we try for perfection in some ways, and I'm just so painfully aware, especially as I get older and I don't keep things in mind or as mindfully as I could be about time, for instance, or sometimes scheduling. I mess up, my office manager messes up. Whoever that is, it's still my responsibility. And I'm very grateful for that chance with her. That's very special to me.

Parent: Thank you. I guess that appointment bothered me so much because that was when I was going to find out what was going on. Like I think if it was a regular therapy session, I would have been like, "Oh, well, no big deal . . . not a big deal." But it was so important to me because I was so worried.

RH: And it's really a gift to other people that you're talking about what this experience has been like for you, for your daughter, in that way. Is there anything you want to say or to ask me to say at this point?

Parent: I feel like through the course of us talking . . . I guess I feel like I see in my daughter what I needed to see and so I don't really have any questions for you because I see the answers in her. And so I don't really have a question because I just . . . I have my daughter back. And she's just front and center like she used to be.

## Discussion

An understanding of one parent's accounting of what sandplay represents for her and her daughter may hold implications for how therapists working with children in sand approach family dynamics—and even help parents and caretakers make sense of the sandplay journey itself. An enlightened parent can foster a positive attitude, not just toward the activity of sandplay in particular, but toward the therapeutic process as a whole. In this instance, the power of sandplay's healing potential was far more important to this mother than the belief that she never gave "second chances." That's a powerful message for us all about listening to, and being guided by, the activation of the child's capacity for healthy emotional development within the sheltering presence of the sandplay therapist.

~

# PART II

# THE CLINICAL USE OF MAPPING THE CHILD HEROINE'S JOURNEY

## *On the Way*

If you ever meet someone brave and powerful enough to walk with you directly through your most unconscious wounds and shadow caves—someone with the stupefying courage to see through the chinks of your armor and then help you take it off—love them because they have done something for you which is impossible to do alone. They will show you the treasure you've been seeking all your life, and they can do this because they aren't afraid of your fear.

Jacob Nordby, *Blessed Are the Weird*
Reprinted with permission

CHAPTER FOUR

~

# Clinical Considerations

## Figuring Out Where Our Clients Are in Their Journeys

When therapists begin to study sandplay or sandtray methods, the question "How do I figure out where my client is in their sandplay process?" becomes paramount; along with a statement such as "I have no idea what is going on here in the trays." Therapists have always been concerned with more fully perceiving where their clients are in terms of the stages of the sandplay journey. Are the clients ready? Are they just beginning? Are they working out conflicts? Are they nearing termination of the therapy? What part do I play in this work as the child's therapist? What is happening here? This is the heart of the matter.

Jane Hirschfeld remarked,

> To ask a good question is a way to carabiner yourself to intimacy, a doorknob that turns only one direction, toward open. . . . It can terrify, bringing you straight into your own fears, whether of heights, or of loss or of all the mysteries that never go away—our own vulnerability, the heart's utter exposure, the capriciousness and fragility of events, of relationships, of existence . . . a way to keep present the awakening question that's under all other questions: "What else, what more?" (*O Magazine*, December 6, 2015).

When viewing the trays of client journeys, it is important to keep several key aspects of the paths our clients choose in mind. One of those is focusing on elements in the journey: the psyche may express itself through different states of water, air, fire, and earth elements. Other systems of analyzing elemental forces such as feng shui (earth, fire, wood, metal, water), the five Chinese elements (fire, earth, metal, water, wood), or the Japanese five elements philosophy (earth, water, fire, wind, void) can also be used to track the use of symbols in these varying elemental states. In this way, tracking symbols can bring out enhanced definition of journey aspects, of the nature of the forces arrayed in conflict. For instance, a child might concentrate on symbols of fire and activation in her initial trays, and seemingly leave out images or miniatures suggesting water, possibly pointing to the challenges of managing unconscious emotional expression and regulation of deep feeling states. Wind may bring in a sense of cognitive processes that sweep the landscape and bring new insights, and stir things up a bit. Fire may indicate activation in one way or another—perhaps anger, maybe heightened awareness, a spark of energy working toward perspective. Working the earth (sand) with construction vehicles or gardening tools may prepare energies and affect for the conflicts and challenges to come to fruition.

The Sandplay Journey Map: Tray Distribution Form for the two case presentations in this book contains a chart of the elements used. It is in no way meant to be a definitive listing of how the elements can be viewed or arrayed. Interpreting sandtrays through the myriad lenses of the varied backgrounds and diversity of the therapists themselves challenges us to see just how many more elemental aspects of the figures and symbols we can appreciate.

Of course, the sand forms the children create are important. The grounding material of the trays is the sand, representative of the earth itself, held in the blue-painted bottom and sides of the trays. Lenore Steinhardt shows these elements and forms in sand in detail in her book *Foundation and Form in Jungian Sandplay* (2000). Other aspects to follow are emotional capacity and mood, presentation of self symbols, themes, whether the symbols appear to be in relationship to each other or not, and regulated or disregulated organizational states of the material used in the trays. The Sandplay Journey Map: Tray Distribution Form also contains room to list up to three self symbols and tray numbers to track the evolution of the client's self-concept over time.

## Working with Young LGBTQ Clients

When Kalff published her clinical casework in 1980, she had been a therapist in Zollikon for over twenty years. Sandtrays by girls in the Swiss environment were dominated by themes of nurturance. Twenty to thirty years later, this clinical finding expanded. Working in sandtrays, Labovitz Boik and Goodwin found that

> as the child transitions [from age] 6–7 to 11–12 years of age, s/he moves into an oppositional stage, with dualities displayed in the tray across or apart from each other. . . . Male and female trays begin to differ significantly, although for both genders there is greater integration of the self than at earlier stages. . . . Girls are more likely to portray individual struggles with opposing forces and often use dangerous animals instead of armed forces. . . . It is not unusual to observe children beginning to include nurturing activities as well as sources of energy in their trays. When a 9-year-old client's trays began changing from our being opponents fighting in the tray to our having a tea party where she prepared and served our meals, it was evident that a shift was occurring (2000, pp. 129–30).

In my experience, each generation seems to try to assert their independence from the previous generation through initiation rites seen as different or "other" from cultural "norms." For instance, symbolic tattoos and piercings have set the millennial generation apart (using a very generalized, diffuse example), which then gets picked up through the larger culture. In the newest generation, the expectation that our children, preteens, and teens expect to be treated as gender fluid appears to be the means by which they are setting themselves apart. This fluidity appears cross-cultural and cross-racial and does not necessarily indicate sexual identity or preference. As our youth work through the challenge of being perceived as whole beings, not identified through gender, we as therapists are subsequently challenged to work with fewer gender stereotypes and expectations. The case presentation of Jess in part IV of this book presents a look at a child of ten who entered therapy identifying as a girl, and subsequently requested to be called by a non-gendered-sounding name, and identified as gender fluid.

At present, Babyatsky-Grayson (2014) notes that

> we do not necessarily have enough information on how to deal with the specific concerns with this population in therapy. . . . It seems that more adolescents and children are coming out as transgender at an earlier age yet it is difficult to know if this is due to better diagnostic developments, biological determinants, or sociocultural acceptance. In spite of this emergence, transgender children and adolescents are still an underserved and poorly researched population that has specific, necessary needs in the mental health and medical arena.

A number of small-n studies indicate that transgender children's rates of depression and anxiety were not significantly elevated when compared with the population average. Although it's hard to generalize, it appears that the children studied whose gender identities were solid and who had strong parental support were in relatively good mental health (Olson, Durwood, DeMeules & McLaughlin, 2016).

Brill and Pepper (2008) delineate stages of gender-nonconforming children from age 2 through adolescence and suggest that transgender identity is "often very clear" by that time. Although at ages 4 through 6, many children "struggle with language to express differences," the authors note that gender-nonconforming children begin to develop self-image problems during this time. Gender-variant and -fluid children may also demonstrate difficulties with social anxiety, shame, confusion, and embarrassment about identity and emotional expression when dealing with outside environments as well as with parents and family members.

Goals of therapeutic intervention with gender-nonconforming children might center around bolstering self-identity (acceptance of feelings and thoughts around body image), appropriate psychological boundaries, and emotional expression with regard to gender and sexual orientation and identity/fluidity. Creating safety in each environment with which the child interacts appears paramount, as is helping to develop self-esteem. Sandplay may be one play therapy approach to assist in a larger context of integrative mental health support and treatment (Goldman, 2014). Bonnie Thomas (2011) published a number of strategies and therapeutic resources geared to the needs of children who do not accept the traditional, more stereotyped gender roles in play and self-concept.

Sandplay uniquely lends itself to sensitively engaging child clients, both verbally and nonverbally, in focusing on their own pathways and self-expression—whether they are gender conforming/nonconforming, gender variant or gender inflexible / gender fluid. As Loue explains, "Through this process, the individual can both discover multiple facets of his or her identity and psyche and examine in greater depth his or her various identities" (2012, p. 105). The difficulty lies with therapist perception and bias, and within the relationships between the parents/family and therapist (and of course within the societal context as well). It is a "must" that we clinicians continually engage in questioning our stance and interactions vis-à-vis our tendency to "judge" what is "acceptable" in terms of gender nonconformity and fluidity in ongoing consultation.

# CHAPTER FIVE

~

# Utilizing the Mandala in the Sandplay Journey Map

## Highlighting Aspects of the Gates

In this chapter we will explore the Sandplay Journey Map and its gateways more fully. We examine the major questions and issues with which our clients struggle.

### Gate 1: Pathways: Choosing to Journey

*Key Terms:* preparation, willingness, choosing to journey, answering "The Call"

*Key Questions:* Is the client willing to undertake this journey right now? Do they have what they need "packed up" for the trip?

*Key Issues:* The client must undertake an internal examination of the psyche and the spiritual connection to "more than oneself," often feeling inadequate, unworthy, and unlovable.

*Major Obstacles:* The client faces the "fear of the unknown," of trusting their inner voice to make the journey, of not getting permission from a parent or guardian to speak about their experience to anyone.

*In this part of the journey, the client decides to undertake her journey to confront, differentiate, analyze, and integrate major conflicts at her stage of development.* In effect, she decides to address her presenting issues within both internal, family, and social contexts.

My favorite story concerning this aspect of readiness and choice in sandplay comes, of course, from inside my sandplay room. One of the children had taken time to work out in play some devastating news about her mother's illness. She was bright, quick, steady, sure. And she noticed that I wanted her to go deeper by using sand. I had said nothing out loud. But I had wondered internally if she might be better served by this modality, rather than what I'd considered the more surface play with which she'd engaged. She certainly knew me well. A glance or two at the trays. Maybe a tightening

The Sandplay Journey Map©: Tray Distribution

(Number the trays sequentially by date and then place the tray numbers into the Gates & Elements below)

Gate 1: Pathways: Choosing to Journey

Gate 2: Discernment: Facing Fear & Embodying Courage

Center ("C"): Illumination: Constellating the Self

Gate 3: Harmony: Reconciling Tensions and Integrating Shadow

Gate 4: Re-Turn: Appreciating Abundance

Elements

____ Fire _____

____ Earth _____

____ Water _____

____ Air _____

1 to 3 Self-Symbol Representations (symbol name/Tray Number)

1. _____

2. _____

3. _____

**Figure 5.1   Sandplay Journey Map: Tray Distribution**

of my lips, or a small resettling in my chair. The field of co-transference we referred to in part I of this book was engaged, and certainly my countertransference as well.

Lena sighed. It was time to share her plan. She pulled up the stool and sat in front of me. She didn't look at my face as she spoke quietly. "You know," she began by saying, "you know that it's like we're in a really great place, like a playground, there's lots of grass and trees all around. And I really like playing here. But it's time to go." "Are you sure?" I asked. "Sure you don't have time to check out some more of the meadow?" "I am," she said. She looked down at her hands. "You see, I know you want to walk further into the woods with me. I know that if I walk and walk, I'll come to a new place. When I get there I'll know it is. And I can hear water nearby." She became silent. "What do you see around you, in that place?" I asked. "Well, it's like there's a wall there, a big one. You can't see over it. The only way to get to the water, to the new place, is to go through the door. It's big, too." "What else does it look like?" I wondered out loud. Her eyes looked into the distance. "It has kind of a window in it, and there's a curtain over it." This time, she looked up into my eyes. "If I go up the steps, if I go up to the window, I know I could see the other side. I know it. But I don't want to." Lena's voice began to rise slightly.

"You know," I said quietly, "that many people never even leave where the trees begin, where the children play. They never walk in the woods, never want to know that there's a door, a wall, water on the other side. You do. You know how to get there." We sat for a bit together, not saying anything. "So," I said, "if you ever want to come back here and see what's behind that curtain, you let your parents know. Or maybe someone else, someday. Someone you can trust. It'll still be there." She snuck another look at me, and nodded. She left the session in her quick, serious, steady way.

I never saw her again. She sent her younger brother to me, a few years later. She told her mother it would be the best thing for him. And he and I had some good times in the sand. And I still wonder . . . will she ever visit that beautiful river, travel through that door? What can I do except smile at that thought?

This part of the gateway includes trays that illustrate the initial stage of the journey. The Sandplay Journey Map presupposes that the client has decided to take the hero or heroine's journey. From that moment on, the client begins the path in the first gateway. This includes, in effect, the client's decision to address his or her presenting issue. With children, there are two types of trays that manifest here: (a) naming trays and (b) "H'neini" trays. The naming trays are about literally writing their name in the sand, or using colored pebbles or tiles or treasured objects to write out their name in the sand.

The "H'neini" tray is one I have named after the story of Moses and Adonai. In this story, Moses had been shepherding his flock and became startled to see a bush burning. It burned and yet was not burned out in the fire. The voice of Adonai spoke from the bush. Moses was the one who needed to go to Pharaoh in Egypt to guide the Israelites to the Holy Land. Adonai had to speak twice to Moses, who was terribly frightened by this experience. Moses didn't want to go and argued that he was too "slow of speech" to do this task, hiding his face with fear and shame. Moses first resisted by questioning "Who am I to go tell them all this?" and then "What would I tell them that your name is?" Adonai responded, "I am that I am." Grudgingly and finally, Moses responded to Adonai by saying: "H'neini" (Here I am).

What is so poignant about this story and about our clients' journey in the sand at this crucial point is that there is so much resistance to answering the call. The story illustrates the need to take responsibility for oneself and one's needs, to pay attention and be present to ourselves (Bridges, 2011). When a client makes this tray, they usually place their hands, sometimes a foot, or one of their initial self-symbol miniatures into the tray as a way of giving themselves a name in the world of the archetypal passage. They may draw in their face or body using treasures or colored stones. This may not be the only time the child places themselves literally into the tray, but it is the first.

After making this type of nonverbal statement—in effect, that the girl client can manifest herself in a visceral way in the tray—she will often begin to prepare for the journey by gathering in her resources and energies. These "gathering the energy" trays frequently use horses to express this rounding up of vibrant power. The horse can manifest as a symbol of instinct and of freedom, of the closely held relationship between rider and horse, of disciplined athleticism and the release of fear. A treatise on this subject can be heard through this link: http://www.npr.org/2011/02/09/133600424/why-do-girls-love-horses-unicorns-and-dolphins

As the client begins to set out, look for a pathway of some kind: sometimes it is clearly defined, other times indistinct or there's just a general indication that there is a journey path.

## Gate 2: Discernment: Facing Fear and Embodying Courage

*Key Terms:* tension of the opposites, shadow aspects of the psyche, discrimination of what's most important, keys to understanding, sacrifice.

*Key Questions:* What is the client most afraid to face? What must the client have to sacrifice in order to get what they need and/or want?

*Key Issues:* The client must handle the challenge of differentiating and confronting ambivalence and tensions; face shadow conflicts and unresolved issues within; battle with aspects of the self; accept help, realize they are not alone.

*Major Obstacles:* The client has difficulty believing in worthiness, being lovable, or the ability to harness resources and strengths.

*Here in this gateway, the client works with separating the opposite emotions of whatever they must face (e.g., love/hate; dependency/independence; mastery/fear; loss / new possibilities), called "the tension of the opposites."* It could also be entitled "Discriminating and Facing the Shadow" or "Meetings and Battles" as well as "Differentiating the tension of the opposites." In many heroic fairy tales and myths, the hero or heroine is not handed the key to understanding their task or perspective in life, but a helper figure points the way to finding the key. At this point in the sandplay journey, these meetings with helpers and inner resources as well as battles with despair, anger, and shadow in the psyche are prominent. This part of the journey is often the most effortful for a client, in terms of the challenges and demands upon psychological hardiness, persistence, and resilience.

Within the second gate, the client works to differentiate and separate the opposite emotions of whatever they must face. When we speak about separating out the tension of the opposites, what does the term mean? "The term *tension of the opposites* refers to the dynamic and often ambivalent strain between two aspects of our nature, our yearnings, our needs—such as love and hate or a belief in one's essential goodness versus one's feelings of worthlessness or inadequacy" (Heiko, 2010, p. 174). Examples of these opposites can be dependency/independence; mastery/fear; new possibilities /

loss; belonging/rejection. Here, clients must engage with two valences of what they want, and what they fear most.

These dual valences can be thought of as "ambi-valence," a play on the word. If we hold out our hands before us, we can demonstrate this. With closed fists I can examine nothing. Stretching out my fingers, palms up I can metaphorically "put" whatever valence of need, desire, fear, into one palm. And then I can do the same with the other palm. I never want to mash those two palms together when acknowledging the challenges of holding those two seemingly diverse emotional states/needs/drives open for examination. Jung spoke about there being

> no consciousness without discrimination of opposites. This is the paternal principle, the Logos, which eternally struggles to extricate itself from the primal warmth and primal darkness of the maternal womb; in a word, from unconsciousness. . . . Nothing can exist without its opposite; the two were one in the beginning and will be one again in the end. Consciousness can only exist through continual recognition of the unconscious, just as everything that lives must pass through many deaths (2014, p. 33).

Marion Woodman has recorded an exposition of "The tension of the opposites" (http://www.soundstrue.com/store/holding-the-tension-of-the-opposites-2201.html). Here we meet with opposing forces in ourselves, conflicting life patterns and experiences of unmet needs and possible trauma and loss. During this gateway, often separating out the tension of the opposites becomes the focal point. We must begin to separate out aspects of shadow and light in ourselves. "The sad truth is that man's real life consists of a complex of inexorable opposites—day and night, birth and death, happiness and misery, good and evil. We are not even sure that one will prevail against the other, that good will overcome evil, or joy defeat pain. Life is a battleground. It always has been, and always will be; and if it were not so, existence would come to an end" (Jung, 1968, p. 75). Can a client accept feeling ambivalently about having that dynamic tension present? Sandplay journeying develops this tension and acceptance through the tray symbolism and progression.

Something has to be sacrificed in the psyche—some tightly held beliefs or memories or perspective—in order for us to continue our journey. Charon, the boatman to Hades on the River Styx, has to be paid in coin; that this costs us in some way opens the path to later acceptance of ourselves and our value in the world.

Our clients choose which doors to open, which way to go. Clients find themselves quite fatigued after a sandplay session when undertaking this phase of the journey. I often offer small protein and complex carbohydrate snacks and drinks to the children to help them learn to regulate their energy reserves, in addition to utilizing the EMDR "buzzies" (handheld tactile pulsars), which can help strengthen focus and mindful attention.

Within this gateway, many of the trays of both boys and girls contain construction sites. Digging and processing the earth becomes a major task. Children often spend time mining the earth for its treasures at this point in the journey as well.

In my work with children, I have noticed that boys tend to work out these conflicts through warriors from different eras or fantasy fighting figures. Pastore (2007) and Hunter (1998) articulated the struggles of boys through the trays: rough, unfinished, terrible in their unfocused rage and despair. Big feelings translate into big energies in the tray. Sometimes children and adults take figures out of the tray after putting them in; or even put them back on the shelf after reaching for them.

Sorting and discriminating are qualities necessary for negotiating this gateway. Girls often demonstrate early boundaries and categorizing behaviors by putting together scenes of farms or animals in the wild, or perhaps making self-trays that explore the dangers of vulnerability and uncertainty.

In sandplay, girls tend to use people or fantasy-figure miniatures (e.g., mermaids, elves, or fairies) to play out relationship struggles in homes, farms, and wooded areas. Fanciful animals (e.g., unicorns, dragons, winged horses) appear in the girls' trays. Frequently, girls will demonstrate internal tensions through verbal fights with characters (real or fantasy) in the trays.

As Simmons so aptly relates: "Girls are deeply relational creatures, whose lives and stories are dominated by the people they sit next to, the parties they go to (or don't), the people they love the most and the ones they can't stand. Girls are like seismographs, sensing the tiniest shifts in their relational landscape" (2009, p. 51). Teen girls frequently use ordinary people miniatures to play out relationship struggles. Teens are most connected to their social network and derive solace and perspective from peer contacts; and their sandplay reflects that.

Von Franz related that a heroine in tales must learn that

> Separating the good from the bad grains is a work of patience, which can neither be rushed into nor speeded up. . . . It is a work of careful, detailed discrimination, but not discrimination as done by the male logos. . . . The feminine principle also has its way of seeing clearly, but it acquires it in a different psychological development, more by the selection of innumerable details, showing that this is this and that is that. . . . By working it out in detail the grains are selected. In a problem of relationship one has to do this all the time. Boring as it is, and gossipy as it seems, a psychological problem cannot be worked out without all these little details. One discovers that women love to be a little unclear, giving rise in that way to those marvelous witch muddles where nobody knows what is what any more. . . . They make a vague arrangement, then a big scene if the thing does not work. . . . The shadow cannot function in the same way if you are precise (1972, p. 217).

During the "working out" of the dynamics inherent in the relationships, the world builder in the sand must stop, take some metaphorical deep breaths, and turn to that aspect of herself. She must ask that internal part of herself—the one that has been ignored, devalued, feared—asking herself: What do you want from me? What can I give you? What do you need? In essence, according to my very wise colleague Sharyn Warren, "What is the pebble in your shoe?" (personal communication, June 30, 2017).

Once someone has "shut down," constructed inflexible armor and gone into metaphorical hiding, how can one open up again? In stories and myths, if you are very lucky, you cross paths with someone who hands you a key in exchange for some assistance. The heroine in these stories must earn this key to understanding their task or perspective in life. In the story of Vasilisa, the girl must work her fingers and her brain furiously and competently to complete the tasks set before her. Toward the end of her time in the Great Hag's hut, she has earned the right to the skull's fire, the key to illumination in the psyche, before she is thrust back out to make her way back home through the forest. "Asking the proper question is the central action of transformation—in fairy tales, in analysis, and in individuation. The key question causes germination of consciousness. The properly shaped question always emanates from an essential curiosity about what stands behind. Questions are the keys that cause the secret doors of the psyche to swing open" (Estes, 1992, p. 48).

Despite the fact that we live in an age where a popular belief insists "you create your own reality," real truth in the form of research and best practice is that sometimes people can't get out of fear or traumatic cycles easily (van der Kolk, 2014; Siegel, 2015). Helpers, protectors, therapists, guardians, elder figures, and mentors are necessities. We can find ourselves hampered by working with partial vision; and someone with greater perspective, skills, or wisdom can come through for us just at the right time. "For me, the form that help often took was that by the grace of the gods, I was given true friends—those who saw me not as I saw myself (an image that came from a house in which I hid), but saw inside to what I truly was and welcomed that being, allowed me to finally see my own essence and bring it into the world. Being truly seen is a gift whose value cannot be overestimated. In the fairy tale, being recognized brings nothing less than resurrection" (Steiber, 2007). Girls need to remember that they are not alone.

The healer archetype may become activated in the psyche during this phase in the form of modern-day figures of Chiron, Hygeia, or Asclepius manifesting in scenes containing hospitals, doctors' offices, veterinarian clinics, or dentist rooms. For girls, opposite from boys, the need to internally represent the animus aspect and energy of the masculine may lead the client to conjure a senex, wizard, or warrior figure, often who appears holding a light or flame or flask. This symbol may metaphorically shine into corners and crevasses in the psyche. Openings in the earth may begin to emerge as well.

Girls frequently turn to grandparents or uncles and aunts or family friends to help them learn about finding a quiet place within to rest and recharge. This is so necessary in order to manage the journey with patience and tenacity. Girl journeys often feature the Dangerous Old Woman archetype (e.g., see Estes, http://www.soundstrue.com/store/the-dangerous-old-woman-641.html, for some exquisite work on this aspect). Goddesses can often appear to both males and females in their journeys (we will see that later on in the case presentation in chapter 8: "A Journey to the Light/"Lainey"). Drawing upon energies of wise elders, fairy godmothers, and the queen herself adds to the girl client's strength and confidence level.

Concentration on the elements of water and fire appear in this gateway. Flooded trays (those containing only water, or bursting with water) or molding wet sand make their appearance at this stage of the journey. Turtles and dolphins, animals that can negotiate both land and sea crossings (otherwise named "psychopomps") can lead the girl clients to new discoveries about themselves. There can be scenes of deep-sea fishing and peering into the bottom of the ocean, the mud near the water's edge, the boundary area between water and earth. It can be that grief fills up the space with salty tears, or that being in water provides rest and liquid calm. "The purpose of the descent as universally exemplified in the myth of the hero is to show that only in the region of danger (watery abyss, cavern, forest, island, castle, etc.) can one find the 'treasure hard to attain' (jewel, virgin, life-potion, victory over death)" (Jung, 1968, p. 335).

To illuminate means to bring the light of our understanding and discrimination to the scene in front of us and around us. We need to help our clients explore their roots, so that they can make sense out of their relationships in the present. Light and fire symbolism often accompanies the world-building of clients when they begin to access the "activation" energies within themselves—whether that be aggressive impulses, anger, frustration—or the life energy, the "juiciness" of the expression of the spirit of the girl within. Too often, girls are taught by family, peers, culture not to express the full range of this often fiery activated energy. Instead of demonstrating a healthy expression of anger or "darker" emotions, these girls respond with sadness. When more fiery symbolism manifests in these trays, we welcome its appearance.

In my sandplay practice, I encourage this expression of activated energies with what I call the "Burning Bowl." Whenever someone uses a match, I save it, and place it in a raku bowl I know I can heat without concern. The bowl is small; and the clients can safely burn paper or matches or stubs of candle inside it to their heart's content within the sandtray boundaries. Many ceremonies and rituals are enacted by the girl clients through this Burning Bowl ritual.

We also need some self-examination during this phase of the journey. The children begin to ask themselves: What characteristics of mine do I enjoy, do I delight in? What irritates me? What qualities hold me back from satisfaction and the courage to do what I must to grow? Often, what is irritating to our clients in our therapist persona is what is most difficult for the client to acknowledge in themselves. One example of this is a child who was severely traumatized, who had gone through a number of therapists unsuccessfully. She indicated through whispers to her mother in the waiting room, that I was not to talk, smile, or laugh. This continued for a full six months, as she tested the boundaries of our safe contract. Her first smile at me was one of the best gifts I have ever received.

When adult clients first consult with me, I gently say that they may find that things I do or say to be uncomfortable or irritating to them at some point—that is, if I'm doing my job properly. We smile at each other; they usually say that this will not happen. I know it will. Sometimes it may be that I ask them to take a deep breath and notice what they are feeling in their body when they want to rush through relating an experience. Or I might miss something in what they said or misremember something. With children, however it manifests—the tension, irritation, or frustration—can lead to a deeper understanding between us when the child is able to be honest about that discomfort. Sometimes that is the Great Work of therapy for the girl clients.

Another aspect of this self-examination is to look at shadow in ourselves and in our lives.

"The *shadow* refers to that internal material that we either don't yet want to face, aren't ready to know about ourselves, or aren't yet capable of understanding and integrating. It doesn't have to do with concepts of evil, really, just those darker denied aspects of ourselves to which we aren't yet reconciled" (Heiko, 2010, p. 174). We need to help our clients explore their roots, the dynamics and early experiences, so that they can make sense out of their relationships in the present.

Often we punish ourselves far beyond childhood or young adulthood far more successfully and enduringly than the original abuse or rejection or neglect by life, our family, or what our circumstances warranted.

Erica Jong wrote a poem that speaks to the viciousness inherent in ourselves as girls and women, which is quoted in part:

**Alcestis on the Poetry Circuit**
(In Memoriam Marina Tsvetayeva, Anna Wickham,
Sylvia Plath, Shakespeare's sister, etc., etc.)

The best slave
does not need to be beaten.
She beats herself.

Not with a leather whip,
or with stick or twigs,
not with a blackjack
or a billyclub,
but with the fine whip
of her own tongue
and the subtle beating
of her mind
against her mind.

For who can hate her half so well
as she hates herself?
and who can match the finesse
of her self-abuse?

Years of training
are required for this.
Twenty years
of subtle self-indulgence,
self-denial;
until the subject
thinks herself a queen
and yet a beggar—
both at the same time.
She must doubt herself
in everything but love . . .

Reprinted with permission

A metaphorical volcano of negative emotions, need, anger, fear, and anxiety can build up in girls, which our culture believes accessing and expressing to be a weakness. "Hence, like a treasure easily discovered in my own house, I must appreciate my enemy as a helper on the path to enlightenment" (Shantideva, 1970, verse VI.107). Yet if girls don't acknowledge the existence of these "darker" emotions, they can end up having explosions of temper, making rash decisions, and feeling a constant, low-level irritability. In sand scenes, marauders in the form of pirates come to garner the spoils for themselves, further depleting girls' vitality. Representations of this volcanic energy manifest during this gateway. As a means of coping, a client may utilize helper figures to rescue her from external and internal harm.

Fencing and caging symbols often appear at this juncture. "And so in the psyche, we cannot 'dispose' of dangerous or destructive aspects of ourselves, we can only know of their presences and how they tend to function. If we work at it we may be able to transform these dark elements from something virulent to something manageable. That is part of the greatness of Jung's concept of the self-regulating nature of the psyche: he never supposed evil could be done away with, but sought to expose and understand the potentiality for evil in our own souls as well as that for good" (Singer, 1994, p. 138).

Separation in the form of images of islands may arise during this gateway. The trays may also contain images of bridges; either without a clear sense of exactly what is to be bridged or, conversely, symbolic representations of opposing forces on either side of the bridge.

## Center: Illumination: Constellating the Self

*Key Terms:* Self, being, spirit, centering, constellation of the self, numinous, treasures

*Key Questions:* Can the client allow themselves to show the beauty, resources, and joyful strength found within the psyche? Will the client feel terrified to face deep fears? Can they accept themselves in their imperfection and with their weaknesses as well as strengths?

*Key Issues:* Clients manifest the beauty of the inner treasures of the psyche and their unique sense of self, demonstrate a need for bravery and strength to demonstrate wholeness, be "in the moment," expressing fully that "I am."

*Major Obstacles:* Fears of "letting go" and of trusting the self, vulnerability, shame.

*This part of the journey could also be called The Celebration of the Light Within, or the Celebration of the Treasure Within.* In this gateway, the client shows themselves the beauty of and connection to the numinous. Sometimes there are many trays in this internal centering process for children in particular, other times only one or two at the halfway point in the progression of trays.

In the center, a girl can celebrate the moment of agency in being able to say to herself: "Yes, I can really do this." Centering trays—not constellation of the self trays—begin to emerge at first. There is a sense of coming to negotiate the belief that the self is worthy, more than adequate, and that the treasures of the deep self deserve to be acknowledged. Many self-symbols begin to appear, connecting the girl to a sense of herself in a positive way. These self-symbols often weave through the tray progression. Examples of these self-symbols may take the form of a starfish as a symbol of a human, the sea star: sacred to Mary, and regenerative symbol, as the starfish can restore an injured part of itself (Heiko, 2008).

Kalff spoke about the sense that comes through to the client who knows she is not alone, who feels seen and heard by the therapist. She recognized that many children have not experienced the necessary protections from adequate parenting, "or because the Self-manifestation has been critically disturbed by external influences such as war, illness, or lack of understanding from the environment during the child's early development" (2004, p. 6). Kalff believed that through her clinical work, there is a "natural tendency of the psyche to constellate itself when a free and sheltered space is created. . . . This psychic situation can establish an inner peace that contains the potential for development of the total personality. This includes its intellectual and spiritual aspects" (p. 7).

Jung expressed the ineffable in relation to constellating the self: "The unrelated human being lacks wholeness, for he can achieve wholeness only through the soul, and the soul cannot exist without its other side, which is always found in a 'You.' Wholeness is a combination of I and You, and these show themselves to be parts of a transcendent unity whose nature can only be grasped symbolically" (1966, p. 454).

When the trays become filled with flowers and gemstones and pretty maidens and princes wandering exquisite gardens, therapists can become entranced by the surface loveliness. "Grossenbacher believes there is often confusion around what constitutes a Self tray. She cautions that beauty alone does not equal a Self tray. She says centering is usually visible, but more important qualities are that it comes from the depths of the psyche, indicates that something has been integrated, and reflects an element of transformation. An internal feeling is aroused, and often a sense of mystery. Sometimes clients will ask for the meaning of the tray. She encourages them to just experience the tray, not to ask why it came at this time, in this way" (Cunningham, 2013, p. 3).

This powerful experience of the numinous for therapists working with children in sandplay was explored by von Gontard (2011). Sometimes there are many trays in this internal centering process for children in particular, other times only one or two at the halfway point in the progression of trays. Children often create birthday party trays, which can contain the "steadying point," the place of numinous centering of the self (Heiko, 2004).

## Gate 3: Harmony: Reconciling Tensions and Integrating Shadow

*Key Terms:* Resolving the "tension of the opposites," integration, synthesis.

*Key Question:* Can the client accept and integrate the most painful, opposing forces in their psyche?

*Key Issues:* Accepting unbearable tensions, demonstrating an integration of conflicts and shadow material into consciousness and harmony within the psyche.

*Major Obstacles:* Clients demonstrate varying ability to accept dynamic tensions as part of the process of balancing values, needs, and the struggles in their lives.

*The trays in this gateway tend to work on resolving conflict, and mediating an acceptance of the tension of the opposites.* Clients continue to reconcile the tension of the opposites and work through psychological conflicts and grief.

In this gateway, clients begin to accept the ambi-valence of the tension of the op-posites, and work through their struggles with renewed strength and vitality. Crossing imagery manifests during this gateway. Images of bridging one aspect of the psyche to another manifest in this gateway as well as in the fourth gateway. Egg and nest symbols herald that the seeding process begun in the second gateway makes way for new beginnings.

Now clients can take possession of the rewards of treasures found in centering, and make them their own. Girls can begin, for example, to find more comfortable and peaceful ways of relating to old enemies, both internal and in the external world of school, family, and social networks. They can demonstrate this in present time or in fantasy.

We revisit Estes's perspective here. She states:

> The way to maintain one's connection to the wild is to ask yourself what it is that you want. This is the sorting of the seed from the dirt. One of the most important discriminations we can make in this matter is the difference between things that beckon to us and things that call from our souls. . . . When we are connected to the instinctual self, to the soul of the feminine which is natural and wild, then instead of looking over whatever happens to be on display, we say to ourselves, "What am I hungry for?" . . . "What do I long for?" . . . This discrimination which Vasilisa learns as she separates poppy seeds from dirt and mildewed corn from fresh corn, is one of the most difficult things to learn, for it takes spirit, will, and soulfulness and it often means holding out for what one wants (1992, pp. 110–11).

The girls working within this gateway must navigate through the sorting process to claim what is useful. In gardening metaphor, we take inventory again of what we have ploughed, seeded, and nurtured during the previous gateways, and prune and counter the destructive effects of all of the external hazards. Amatruda and Helm Simpson effectively addressed this gardening metaphor for perspective-taking over the course of the sandplay process (2008). What might this mean for a girl client? Perhaps in "taking stock" of what she has learned over the course of the journey, in this gateway, she can appreciate the burgeoning qualities she's found in herself. These are the quali-ties of resourcefulness, strength, self-confidence, steadiness—as well as her own sense of what pathway she would like to choose next to follow.

Additionally, embracing the parts of ourselves that we have cut off, refused to acknowledge or accept, is key to moving through the journey with confidence. Girls also need to nourish that internal part that forms the animus aspect. In a woman, for instance, this can be seen in images of a young male, who grows up through the tray progression and journey. With a girl client, this might take the form of watching a wild tiger cub figure flow into a tame kitten and then evolve into a strong male dog symbol (Heiko, 2008). Often an observing ego shares perspective in symbols that let the world-builder gain height (e.g., utilizing ladders, steps, tall trees forts, giraffes, or lookout towers).

For the most part, girls know how to hold pain and handle suffering close in the body and heart. They are socialized to find crying acceptable, but not tantrums or yelling. The hardest part is in allowing herself to tolerate anger without falling into sadness: to grow the skill of patience with shadow emotions and just leave that space open for new energies to come at some future point. Symbolic representations of humor and trickster energy abound in this gateway. Being more open to humor and laughter in the co-transference relationship allows this aspect of perspective-taking to continue to take root.

Images of the Sacred Marriage, the Hieros Gamos, occur during this phase of the journey. At this place, learning to balance the opposites with grace and acceptance becomes vital. Balance is not staying steady in one place, although that can be quite an accomplishment at times. It is the attitude and ability to negotiate the elements of life with an internal stillpoint. Kalff knew this well, stating that one of the children with whom she worked "no longer had to choose 'one or the other.' Now that he had experienced both, he could live with one and the other"—in other words, working through the conflict to the integration of the opposites (2004, p. 135).

Clients in sandplay often go too far from their birthplace to bring back hard-won perspective and knowledge. Girls in the United States often choose miniatures from across the world to place in the trays: a Torii gate, Asian mud fishermen, cities from Europe and Asia, animals in the savannah. In *La Prisonnière*, Marcel Proust said, "A pair of wings, a different respiratory system, which enabled us to travel through space, would in no way help us. The only true voyage . . . would be not to visit strange lands but to possess other eyes, to see the universe through the eyes of another, of a hundred others, to see the hundred universes that each of them sees, that each of them is" (Bales, 2001, p. 196). In this gateway, the pieces of the puzzle of diversity are woven together.

Here, girls work to integrate the lost parts of themselves, the parts they hadn't time, energy, or interest in forging, sometimes manifesting, this synthesis in self trays. More abstract trays may appear in this gateway, representing the Mystery; or using forms of sand or representations of color, shape, or texture.

## Gate 4: Re-Turn: Appreciating Abundance

*Key Terms*: "Return to the Collective," coming home to everyday life, appreciating the vitality and "juiciness" inherent in life.

*Key Question*: Is the child capable of taking the treasures of understanding, which they worked so hard to discern, back into everyday life?

*Key Issues:* Clients must try to carry the insights from the journey back for use in everyday life, learn to enjoy the wisdom and the fruits of their efforts, and take time to "smell the roses."

*Major Obstacles:* Clients frequently demonstrate difficulty adjusting to the inflated sense of self manifested by constellating the self. The client must relativize the insights gleaned from the journey. It can be a challenge to accept that we return again and again in greater understanding and perspective to the conflicts and struggles we face—that we continually must rework our experiences, our narrative in the spiral journeys of life. This can be exhausting to contemplate.

*This gateway represents an integration of the psychological material worked through in the journey, and a relativistic return to everyday life.* Sandtrays manifest by becoming more realistic in nature. Often there are fewer trays in this gateway.

This gateway represents the process of coming to equilibrium in the psyche, which is represented by activities of daily life. Clients in this gateway can more easily accept joyful moments and allow themselves to feel the connection to their heart and in "being with" others.

There is a *niggun*, a Hebrew chant, that says: "Return again, return again, return to the land of your soul, return to who you are, return to what you are, return to where you are, born and reborn again." This chant is sung until the singer finds herself in a trance of peaceful reflection. This mirrors the easeful connections that can be found in the fourth gateway.

Now sandtrays might become more realistic; or, since we are focusing on children, can represent this level of confidence and strength in abstractions. Ascent and harmonious imagery now defines and consolidates this final part of the spiral journey. Here is where girls can experience the fullness of having enough in their lives, after the unsettling and painful resolution of many struggles and wounding. A girl can bring the treasure of perspective and insight back to the place she lives and she then "becomes a member of the collective" (Kalff, 2004, p.10).

This is the place where clients continue to work on refining what they have learned through their sandplay journey, "bringing it on home." Just as wood is reworked and retooled, so the sandplay path brings the client to a "re-turn," again and again in the spiral journey.

I have found that using this method of scrutinizing the client's work in the sand deeply enriches our perspective in terms of which aspect of the Journey the client finds him or herself. It is an invaluable tool for training therapists in the sandplay model. As the saying goes, "Anyone can plant a seed, but only a farmer can make it grow." It's lovely to help our clients "cultivate" the trays and bring forth its treasures to be shared.

~

# PART III

# APPLYING THE SANDPLAY JOURNEY MAP TO THE ENCHANTED STORY OF "VASILISA THE BRAVE"

## Awakening and Initiation

To heal you must remember who you really are. Then no matter what happens to you, you can rely on this innate courage, you can trust your own wise heart because nothing and no one can take that from you.

Jack Kornfield (2014, pp. 8–9)

CHAPTER SIX

~

# An Example of a Girl Heroine's Journey through Fairy Tale

There is a rich and varied understanding of the nature and analysis of the use of fairy tales. According to von Franz, "Fairy tales are the purest and simplest expression of collective unconscious psychic processes. Therefore their value for the scientific investigation of the unconscious exceeds that of all other material. They represent the archetypes in their simplest, barest, and most concise form. In this pure form, the archetypal images afford us the best clues to the understanding of the processes going on in the collective psyche. In myths or legends, or any other more elaborate mythological material, we get at the basic patterns of the human psyche through an overlay of cultural material. But in fairy tales there is much less specific conscious material, and therefore they mirror the basic patterns of the psyche more clearly" (1996, p. 1).

Scholars Marina Warner, Jack Zipes, and Maria Tatar, to name a few, have examined the interpretation of these tales in popular culture within the context of the ancient traditions of storytelling to the present day. Of course, some fairy tales are just rollicking great stories that would defy an organized or dynamic understanding. To Warner, who has spend a lifetime pondering them, fairy tales are "stories that try to find the truth and give us glimpses of greater things." . . . Warner documents the process of meaning-making over time vis-à-vis fairy tales. . . . If, by the term "psychological," we mean relevance for mental life in its entwined cognitive and affective functioning, we are right to invoke it here, for fairy tales speak directly and indirectly to the psyche. They stimulate rainbows of feeling, insatiable curiosity, and inexhaustible searches for meaning (Spitz, 2015).

Bruno Bettleheim, a psychoanalyst, examined the meaning of using fairy tales therapeutically for children within the context of an Oedipal viewpoint. Murray Stein and Marie-Louise von Franz, both Jungian analysts, have written extensively about the interpretation of fairy tales by amplifying symbolic and metaphorical meanings within a Jungian context. Von Franz believed that in order to handle the issue of evil in our lives, we must manage to follow their guidance in "rules of behavior on how to cope" using their "natural wisdom" (1995, pp. 191–92). There is a higher understanding of human nature that can be gleaned from these tales, she suggests, something of great subtlety intricately woven into the smallest details carried within the story's framework. She clarifies by saying,

> That is the difference between a man and a girl's way of treating the Baba Yaga [the Great Witch of the Forest]. . . . The girl is an absolutely helpless young creature. But it also shows here that the Baba Yaga is not evil at all; she is just plain nature. If you know how to cope with her, she is all right. It's up to you which side of her you experience, and here come the first intimation in these stories that . . . evil is not only a nature [sic] phenomenon, but is dependent on man's attitude and behavior. . . . It is in a tiny conversation, just a few sentences of the story, that the whole problem of good and evil is decided. It means walking on the razor's edge to be able to say the right thing, or have the right reaction at the crucial moment, for that turns the whole problem (p. 204).

To best illustrate the concept of journeying, we'll begin with a fairy tale that eloquently speaks to the inner journeying of the girl. We'll work within the frame of the tale of "Vasilisa the Brave." This is a Russian story about the importance for girls of listening to intuition, to that small, quiet voice inside the self. It is a story of courage, of the ability to discriminate what is important through intuition to guide us to the treasure of inner wisdom, of inner "knowing," as well as using the innate resources within us to confront challenges to our safety and well-being.

Vasilisa confronts the terrible aspect of Mother Nature, the Witch of the Forest, who in this incarnation is called Baba Yaga.

> One sees, therefore, that actually the great battle between life and death, good and evil, the girl and the great nature witch, becomes a secret magical contest as to whose magical powers are stronger, the girl's or the great witch's, and the two respect each other's power mutually. Vasilisa does not ask the last question about the witch's secret, and the witch either does not notice, or pretends not to notice, the girl's great secret. So they can part *partie remise* [game postponed] (von Franz, 1995, p. 192).

Although many of these stories were initially shared by storytellers with adults by firesides, this tale is especially vital for girls in terms of strengthening the young feminine aspect of intuition and trusting the inner sense of knowing. "Intuition is the treasure of a woman's psyche," says Estes.

> To my mind, the old Russian tale "Vasilisa" is a woman's initiation story with few essential bones astray. It is about the realization that most things are not as they seem. As women we call upon our intuition and instincts in order to sniff things out. We use all our senses to wring the truth from things, to extract nourishment from our own ideas, to see what there is to see, know what there is to know, to be the keepers of our own creative fires, and to have intimate knowing about the Life/Death/Life cycles of all nature (1992, p. 71).

We go to the heart of a forest, and the indifferent and immense power of the archetype of Mother Nature's energy itself. Vasilisa, our heroine, believes it imperative to follow an uncertain path into the forest to meet the Witch and make a demand to help her stepfamily. She must go through initiation trials, doubt, and terror to find the core of truth and let go of innocence and naiveté. Steiber says of these tales that they offer "a map for getting through to the other side . . . [and] travel to a new state of being. It's worth noting that in the fairy tales the heroine must go to the center of the forest and bring back the treasure of whatever was confronted in that place, coming back out into the world with new perspective, with the wisdom of that journeying" (2007).

There is a rhythm to this primal tale. We find the problem of an abusive step-mother; a flight into the woods; a confrontation with the power of the Baba Yaga; three trials and rituals of initiation; the courage to trust one's own intuition; the blessings of the Mother; following the deep path out of the wood carrying the light of Truth; a confrontation with cold evil leading to death; the destruction of evil through fire; and finally the growth of hope, self-confidence, and individuation through the power of love and connection. The illumination this story brings to our understand-ing of every girl's journey can be powerful.

In a certain Tsardom, in the thrice-nine kingdom, in a small house outside the village near the forest, there lived a trader, his wife, and their daughter. The girl was rosy-cheeked, sweet, and merry. If you met her, you'd see how she danced about, enjoying life and laughing.

Her name was Vasilisa. One day when the father was working far away, her mother became seriously ill. As Vasilisa wept over her mother's hands on the cover of the bed, her mother whispered a secret. Her mother, Vasilisa's grandmother, had gifted the mother with a doll, a tiny little doll. She instructed the mother to always keep the doll close to her heart, tucked into a shirt or a dress pocket. Vasilisa was told that if she gave the doll a bit of bread and a bit of water, the doll would talk to her and help her if ever she found herself in need. Vasilisa's mother blessed her daughter, and tucked a curl behind the girl's ear. Soon after, the mother died.

Vasilisa's father became lonely and in the course of such things, remarried. The woman who took her mother's place came with two daughters who seemed . . . fairly nice. But if you looked closely, you could see that their eyes were narrow and their faces pinched. Their souls were mean and as black as their hearts. For the stepmother was a witch, although not a very good one, one would be afraid to say. When Vasilisa's father was out of the house, the stepmother and stepsisters treated Vasilisa quite badly. The more Vasilisa tried to be helpful and kind, the more cruel the stepmother and stepsisters became. No task seemed too much for Vasilisa, but her kindness and sweet nature shone out of her eyes as she cleaned and cooked and ran errands. The more she asked what she could do for her stepmother and stepsisters, the angrier and meaner they became.

So it came to pass that Vasilisa's father needed to travel to conduct his business in another town. Vasilisa's stepmother decided that this would be a good time to get rid of her unwanted stepdaughter. She cast a spell on the candles and fire in the house, and soon it became quite dark outside and inside the house near the forest. The evil stepmother cried out to Vasilisa to go into the forest and bring back light from the Baba Yaga, the Old Witch of the Forest, and save them all so that they could make a fire to heat the house and cook. "For you know how scared your sisters and I are of the forest animals and such. Only you could save us!"

Without complaint, Vasilisa set out into the forest. She brought the tiny doll, a bit of food, and a goatskin of water. There was no moon to guide her, and soon she became quite lost. She sat down on a log and began to cry. Then she remembered what her mother told her about the doll. The one her mother said to carry next to her heart, always. And so Vasilisa gave the doll a bit of her bread and a drop or two of her water. The doll smiled, and told Vasilisa to steady herself and walk ahead on the path. Whenever Vasilisa became confused about which direction to go, the doll would whisper, "Go to the left," "Go to the right," or "Keep going." And Vasilisa did. She walked all that dark night through the forest.

As Vasilisa walked on, a faint light shone out from the stars. And she heard the wind move strongly near her. As dawn approached, a fierce rider dressed all in white, seated on a white horse, galloped by her. She continued to walk deeper, deeper into the forest through the winding paths. As the sun's light began to sift through the trees, another rider traveled past her, one dressed all in red, on a red steed. The doll continued to comfort her and whisper words of encouragement and tenderness. As the day began to wear on, the path began to widen. Vasilisa had walked all night and most of a day. There was a clearing before her.

The sight that greeted Vasilisa was great and terrible. She saw a hut, standing on chicken feet, which moved to face the waning light. The gates and fences were made of human bones, the bones of hapless visitors the Baba Yaga had eaten! Human skulls sat on top of each of the bones, their eye sockets beginning to glow in the darkness. Human hands formed the hinges of the gates. As night came to the forest, a rider dressed all in black, mounted on a black horse, rode by her. Vasilisa wondered for a moment who all these riders were.

Suddenly the great wind began to rise up and twirl the branches around the trees in the clearing around the hut. From the sky, the Baba Yaga sailed to the earth in a huge mortar, steering it with her pestle. The hut's chicken legs bent down low to the ground, bowing to the Baba Yaga. The Old Hag grinned, showing her fearsome iron teeth sharpened to points. She got out of the mortar, waved her broom around, and shouted, "What took you so long?" Vasilisa was too polite to show surprise. She curtsied, just as her mother had shown her. She stammered out: "My stepmother sent me to get fire to keep the hearth and candles lit, if you please, ma'am." The Baba Yaga laughed again, a horrible, grating sound, and said she knew the witch who was her stepmother, oh, yes, she did.

"Well, I don't give something for nothing, myshka moya. Little mice don't last long here," she cackled, spittle flying everywhere. "You'll have to cook my dinners and do a few little tasks for me. Then you might get your fire. Or I might eat you!" Vasilisa shivered in terror, and carefully picked her way through the yard, following the witch into the hut. They say "fear has big eyes," and Vasilisa's eyes were enormous.

They entered the hut, and Vasilisa saw that a huge oven occupied a great space. The Baba Yaga yelled for Vasilisa to fetch her supper, and to hurry, saying "Ohhhh! Such feasting I will make. The grease will run down my chin, and I will crack your bones with my iron teeth to suck the marrow from within!" Vasilisa set the table quickly with enormous meat pies, pirogies, plates of roasted salmon, vats of borscht, blinis, pelmeni dumplings, giant loaves of rye, buckwheat stew, jugs of red wine and beer. The fearsome Baba Yaga ate everything, picking her teeth with the meat bones.

Then the Baba Yaga smoked a pipe, and the smoke curled around her lined face. She thundered, "Tomorrow you will do the chores. Clean the oven and sweep out this house so it sparkles. Do the cooking for my dinner as well. And one more thing . . . look out this window. See that pile of dirt?" Vasilisa looked at the dark outside, and saw that there was an immense mountain of earth illuminated by the skulls' light across the yard. "There are poppy seeds mixed in that dirt. Hee Hee! Separate them into two piles . . . or you'll be eaten tomorrow night along with my supper!" She immediately curled up on her gigantic bed, and fell fast asleep, snoring mightily. In fear, Vasilisa stared, trembling, at the Old Hag. After a while, she remembered the doll and gave the tiny figure a bit of the rye bread and some water. Vasilisa put her head down and rocked with quiet sobs. She heard a small noise from her pocket over her heart and looked in. The doll shushed her. "Now, now, calm yourself. The morning is always wiser than the evening. Tomorrow you can sweep and clean and cook. I'll take care of the pile of dirt and seeds. Don't you worry. Remember: The morning is always wiser than the evening." Vasilisa went to an uneasy sleep.

In the morning, after the white rider and the red rider passed through the clearing, the Baba Yaga snorted herself awake and cackled to herself, muttering that she'd dine well that night. With that, the Baba Yaga flew up the chimney of the hut with chicken feet and disappeared into the sky in her mortar and pestle.

Vasilisa began to clean and cook. True to her word, the doll accomplished the impossible. When Vasilisa looked out the window after her tasks, there were two piles out in the yard, one of earth, one of poppy seeds. The door to the hut flew open as the first stars began to shine, and the black rider on the black horse rode through the clearing. The Baba Yaga burst into the room. She rubbed her hands together, saying "Well, well . . . I shall crack your bones and feast on the . . . What?" she roared. "What's this?" The Old Hag had just looked out the window and caught sight of the two neat piles, one of earth and one of poppy seeds. Seeing this, she screamed and fussed.

Soon, the Baba Yaga bade Vasilisa bring her a large bowl of the poppy seeds and set it on the table. Vasilisa served up an excellent feast once again, prepared by her own trembling hands, soothed by her doll's help. After dinner, the Old Hag clasped her pipe between her teeth and clapped her hands three times. Suddenly, two pairs of ghostly hands unconnected to anything hovered over the bowl of poppy seeds and squeezed all of the oil out of the seeds. Vasilisa's mouth hung open at the sight.

The Old Hag then tasked Vasilisa to do everything she'd done the day before for the next day; but this time, Vasilisa was to separate a humongous pile of rotten corn kernels from a mountain of robust corn. The Baba Yaga again curled up and grunted and snorted through the rest of the night. Vasilisa fed the doll and was comforted once more when the doll said: "The morning is always wiser than the evening," and told the girl she would take care of the corn. Vasilisa then fell deeply into sleep. She was exhausted.

The next morning, the Old Hag awoke and flew up the chimney of the hut with chicken feet and disappeared into the sky in her mortar and pestle after the white rider and the red rider passed through the clearing. Vasilisa again completed the household tasks and the cooking. When she looked outside the window much later that afternoon, there were two piles, one of rotten corn and one of hardy corn out in the yard. No sooner had she turned away from the window, when the Baba Yaga banged open the door of the hut, screaming for her supper, furious that there were two separate piles of corn visible in the yard. Outside the window, the black rider on a black horse could be seen galloping across the clearing. Again supper was served and voraciously consumed. The Old Hag tasked Vasilisa to again to do everything she'd done the day before. And this time, the girl needed to separate the wheat from the chaff in the colossal pile outside in the yard. The Old Hag slumped over, fast asleep with a belly full of food. She snored the whole night long. Again the doll reassured Vasilisa with the words "The morning is always wiser than the evening," and the girl's eyes slowly closed. In spite of her fear of being eaten, Vasilisa slept deeply.

The next morning, the Old Hag again awoke. She flew up the chimney of the hut with chicken feet and disappeared into the sky in her mortar and pestle after the white rider and the red rider passed through the clearing. At the end of the day, after the black rider on the black horse passed through to the other side of the forest, the Baba Yaga returned. She flattened the door of the hut in her haste to gloat over what she thought would be a weeping little mouse of a girl, her eyes squinting through the window at the two piles of wheat and hulls outside in the yard.

The Old Hag smiled a fearsome smile, her iron teeth glinting in the firelight of the well-tended hearth. "Well. Well. Well. You have done everything I asked. What are you standing around, looking at? As a special boon, a favor to you . . . ask me anything. Don't you want to ask me something?" At this, the doll began to jump up and down in Vasilisa's pocket, trying to get her attention. But Vasilisa didn't heed the doll. She was grateful for the opportunity to ask about the three forest riders in the clearing: the white rider, the black rider, and the red rider. When she did ask about the riders' identities, she was told by the Old Hag that the white one was "my Daybreak," the red one was "my Sun," and the black one was "my Night."

Getting such a fine answer as that was wonderful! The Old Hag owned the sun, the night, all of it! Vasilisa began to ask about those mesmerizing, disembodied hands, the ones that wrung out the oil from the poppy seeds. Now that was something! But the little doll quivered and jumped around in her pocket. Vasilisa quickly realized that enough was enough, and told Baba Yaga she had no further questions. The Baba Yaga cackled with no little disappointment. "For if you had asked me another question, I would have eaten you, myshka moya! Too many questions, it makes me old! No one lives who asks about what happens inside this hut!"

The Baba Yaga cocked her head. "I have a question for you, girl. How did you know to finish all the work I gave you? Well? Speak up!" she ordered. Vasilisa hesitated, then smiled a little and said, "By my mother's blessing, if you please." At that, the Baba Yaga, who wanted nothing to do with blessings, screamed and ground her teeth and sent Vasilisa packing. The Old Hag picked a skull off the fence, placed it hastily on a stick and thrust it into Vasilisa's quaking hands, shouting "Be off with you, girl!"

Vasilisa backed out of the yard quickly and turned to begin her journey back through the deep dark of the forest. As she walked, the skull's burning sockets lit the path ahead of her. Her arm and hand began to shake and grow heavier and heavier. She thought of putting the skull down. No sooner did that thought cross her mind, when the skull's mouth began to hiss strongly to her. "Do not let go of the sssssstick. Hold it sssssteady!" Startled, but obeying the skull, Vasilisa walked on. In the forest she saw everything. She saw animals searching for food, mating, tending their young, fighting, playing, and peeking out of their burrows and holes. On and on she trudged. A few hours more, and through the darkness, she spied the house of the stepmother.

Her stepmother and stepsisters had been waiting and waiting for her return. They had been unable to light a candle or start a fire on the hearth since she left. The reach of the Old Hag is great. They were hungry, cold, and desperate. They surrounded her, grasping with greedy hands for the light. And yet . . . and yet . . . the skull burned even more brightly, and they fell back, terrified. The skull burned high and bright as Vasilisa held it up, and its eyes followed the women wherever they went, even as they hid. By morning, her stepmother and stepsisters were burned to a crisp. Only the ashes were left, and those she buried, along with the skull. Vasilisa continued to have many adventures, and ended up marrying the Tsar, but that is another story for another time.

When Vasilisa's father returned home after many years, father and daughter were happily reunited. We were all there at the palace dinner, and everyone talked of the nastiness and evil of the witch and her daughters. We ate and drank up and had a merry time, especially the doll and Vasilisa. And everyone lived as happily as they could; and they may be there still, or not.

## Twelve Critical Aspects of the Tale

The following are some of the significant aspects of Vasilisa's story. The more we understand how to amplify the symbols and their meanings inherent in the tale, the better we will be able to discern how to apply the Sandplay Journey Map to the story.

1. *The Mother's Blessing*: Here, the symbolism of an empty bed represents the loss of the Mother's guidance, the undifferentiated, naive state of Vasilisa's earlier, protected childhood. The Mother leaves the gift of the doll and the means to receive answers to life's obstacles using her intuition. That is the secret of the mother's blessing.

> Whereas Cinderella and her folkloric cousins usually receive assistance from nature (trees, fish, brooks) or from a fairy godmother, Vasilisa is given a cultural artifact, a figure that can be seen as a miniaturized version of herself or as a symbolic form of her mother. While the doll protects and helps Vasilisa, it is also something to be nurtured and cared for, thus strengthening the fact of her own agency in escaping from villainy at home (Tatar, 2002, p. 173).

This may also represent the wish for the "magic mother"—but in this way, the girl can carry this comfort and perspective with her throughout her lifetime.

If we give the doll a little bread, a little water . . . what does this represent in the psyche? This is the aspect in the psyche that comforts as well as includes the power of discrimination of what is necessary for survival. This is our symbolic ally within: what we can count on, what sustains us on a daily basis. We must remember to be patient, to breathe, to deepen the connection with the internal and the spiritual, continuing to work on listening to our inner voice. It only needs a little sustenance to engage with us.

2. *Vasilisa's Evil Stepmother and Stepsisters*: The Stepmother is the catalyst who forces Vasilisa to break her pattern of innocence and almost too generous "niceness," beginning the Journey into the Forest to find the Great Baba Yaga.

The stepmother forces Vasilisa to work outdoors, where the sun represents the greatest threat to her "fairness," hoping that her complexion will be spoiled. She compares Vasilisa unfavorably to her stepsisters, belittling her. She is the dark aspect of the mother who died, the one who cannot bear to handle the competition of a younger, more accomplished and beautiful girl.

*Unwarranted adoration*: What is it like for a stepdaughter to have to experience the jealousy of the stepmother/mother in terms of her developing body, at the threshold of new choices and life? And her stepsisters, seemingly her friends but actually her enemies. Women's later friendships, often based on early relationships with our personal mother and sisters, are often fraught with control, aggression, jealousy, fear in their more negative aspect. How can we negotiate this safely?

*Claiming authentic power*: As girls and women, we are constantly being challenged to agree to take care of more and more people (e.g., those we love, or those to whom we feel an obligation or duty). Girls and women are frequently anxious about not being of service to others, not putting others first, angering other people or getting into conflict with them. What early bargain did we make in our family for love and rewards? When do we decide to say "No"? How do we save our psychological energy for ourselves? We must ask ourselves, Is it alright to be selfish? What's the cost to our inner psyche?

3. *Vasilisa Listens to Her Doll*: This is the representation of the heroine in her still-innocent, good-girl posture, learning to listen and care for her intuitive voice in the form of the doll. Again, we focus upon the idea that just the tiniest morsel of bread, a sip of water, a bit of attention brings this intuitive inner voice to life.

4. *Making Her Way through the Dark Forest of Birches*: In Vasilisa's native land, the birch represents initiation, growth, renewal, stability, and adaptability—and is able to sustain harsh conditions.

The birch tree is sacred in Russia. It has great resonance for the story of Vasilisa: initiation, growth, renewal, stability, adaptability. It has been associated with the duality of lunar and solar aspects. "The birch symbolizes the path by which energy comes down from Heaven and human aspirations rise up in return" (Chevalier &

Gheerbrant, 1997, p. 86). The birch is able to sustain harsh conditions and is the first growth to repopulate areas damaged by forest fires. It is an excellent igniter as it burns even when damp and is a fire starter over most other woods. It is referred to as the "bright" tree, a reference to its chalky-white bark.

5. *My Daybreak, My Sunset, and My Knight*: Baba Yaga controls nature itself. Each of the Knights is representative of one aspect of nature: the Red Knight and his blood-red horse depicts the dawn; the White Knight and his horse, the sun, characterizing daytime; and the Black Knight astride his coal-black horse, the night. They are hers, and she keeps them at the foot of her great bed in a trunk.

6. *The Hut on Chicken Feet in the Witch's Clearing*: This represents that fertile place where consciousness resides within the middle of the Dark Forest. One must work very hard to reach this place, to trust that inner voice.

The hut of the Dangerous Old Woman is a house that can expand or contract according to what mood she's in or what she wants to teach, and can turn to face the sun at all times during the day.

7. *Baba Yaga Arrives*: She flies in her mortar with a pestle bone to greet Vasilisa, deep in the woods.

> Baba Yaga's domain is the forest, widely acknowledged as a traditional symbol of change and a place of peril, where she acts as either a challenger or a helper to those innocents who venture into her realm. In Western tales, these two roles are typically polarized, split into different characters stereotyped as either "witch" or "fairy godmother." Baba Yaga, however, is a complex individual: depending on the circumstances of the specific story, she may choose to use her powers for good or ill (Pilinovsky, 2004, p. 4).

In this tale, The Old Hag is a cannibal (i.e., remember that fence consisting of skulls). She rides on an implement (broom) used for household labor, and uses it to sweep away her tracks. A healthy appetite implies strength. She is divine; she commands the heavens, the elements. She is the Great Mother in her Dark Aspect. If Vasilisa can pass the tests she sets, fine; but she will devour the girl if the tasks are not completed to her satisfaction.

8. *The Three Sorting Tasks: Sorting Poppy Seeds from Dirt, Healthy Corn Kernels from Rotten Corn; and Wheat from the Chaff*: These tasks symbolize Vasilisa's growing ability to discriminate what is important and what to discard. These tasks require discernment, courage, flexibility, perseverance, self-discipline, determination, and a bit of sneakiness. As Vasilisa sorts, she begins to mature in judgment and skill. She continues to rely on the doll for assistance.

Intuition is actually a part of a cognitive discriminatory function, one of "rapid cognition" based upon unconscious thought processes that occur outside of rational decision making (Hogarth, 2001; Koch, 2015; Weinerman, 2005).

9. *The Mysterious and Disembodied Hands Which Represent the Mysteries of Life and the Unanswerable*: The Baba Yaga cries out, "My faithful servants! Grind up my wheat!

Press the oil out of my poppy seeds!" When Vasilisa stops herself from asking too many questions, she is rewarded by the Old Hag of the Forest telling her that "Every question does not lead to good. If you know too much, you will grow old too soon." According to some versions of this story, the Great Witch ages a year every time someone asks her a question, which just irritates her. There are just some things that must be left alone. Vasilisa is wise enough by this time to know this.

10. *Vasilisa Answers the Baba Yaga: By the Blessing of the Mother*: "I want no blessings here!" the Old Hag screams at Vasilisa, seemingly furious at the mention of a loving personal mother. And, here is the wisdom: the Old Witch of the Forest will not delve into the girl's secret because Vasilisa didn't let her curiosity about the Mysteries of the Baba Yaga's house become too insistent. Both respected each other's secrets (von Franz, 1995).

11. *Vasilisa Brings the Light Back Home: Holding up the Light of Consciousness*: The skull becomes heavier and heavier to carry. There are girls who have felt so betrayed and lost that they just want to give up and hurt themselves (i.e., by cutting a wrist or an ankle) or even attempting suicide. How do we handle this in our life journey? Do we take time to grieve our loss of innocence, of naiveté, and celebrate our mature, more sophisticated nature as we grow, as we continue to make mistakes? How do we keep going?

When we gather the light of the skull, its weightiness emphasizes that we must bear the light of illuminating the shadow aspect of the "full catastrophe of life." What prevents us from illuminating that part of the Self that we don't yet wish to confront? Who holds the light? Who owns the light? Wisdom is what works to preserve things that can't be allowed to perish—the soul, spirit, mind, body, the heart.

12a. *Returning Home with the Burning Light of Truth: The Light Renders Three Black Cinders*: The discerning Light of Truth illuminates and then burns away what is useless, negative, and unnecessary to continuing a creatively satisfying life.

12b. *Enjoying the Fruits of Our Creativity: Vasilisa the Weaver and Her Tsar Bridegroom*: As an adult woman, Vasilisa learns to weave exquisitely and comes to the attention of the Tsar, who comes to love her Illuminated Self. Union with the Beloved leads to forgiveness, acceptance, and the joining in the *hieros gamos*, the Sacred Marriage in the Self.

### Experiential Exercise: Outlining the Tale Using the Sandplay Journey Map

Before we move to this next stage in understanding the Journey Map, let's undertake a sorting task by paging to the Sandplay Journey Map: Tray Distribution Form found on page 34. Try to outline Vasilisa's journey on the form yourself, as if this story were the narrative in a sandplay case presentation. You can use the image names created for this book, as well as your own names for the steps in the gateways.

**Application of the Sandplay Journey Map to the Tale
of Vasilisa the Brave**

Now, let's go back over the important aspects of the Journey Map, using the four gates and center as our guide, as well as your own construction of the task. I have adapted Arrien's gates (2007) to assist with analyzing the Sandplay Journey Map. So, each gate and the center of the mandala of the Journey Map takes this form:

a. the setup of the situation as we find it in the gateway;
b. the gift of understanding this pathway provides;
c. the challenges it requires;
d. a reflection on what has been learned; and
e. suggestions for practice.

You may compare your completed map to the gateways below.

**Gate 1: Pathways—The Path through the Dark Forest**

*The Setup*: The girl chooses to go to the hut of the Baba Yaga to get fire to help her stepmother and stepsisters.

*The Gift*: Her devotion to her mother, her kindness, and her ability to remember to listen to her doll.

*The Challenge*: To be mindful of the doll's wisdom, to remember to take heart from the blessings of being loved, remembering that we are not alone.

*Reflections*: The girl was not forced out on the journey, but chose to do so out of the kindness of her heart, possibly because she feared the stepmother, and the cold and dark as well.

*Practice*: (1) Reflect on how different each journey tale begins for girls in different developmental stages, grades, or maturity levels; and (2) How difficult it is to start out on a journey when fear and anticipation of the dangers ahead accompany us. Can you think of a client right now who is struggling in this way? What might she require in terms of preparation for the journey?

**Gate 2: The Hard Work of Negotiating for the Light**

*The Setup*: The girl meets the Old Hag and negotiates for the light.

*The Gift*: The girl knows hard work and uses the doll (her intuition) to solve the three problems the Baba Yaga sets for her: the poppy seeds, the corn, the wheat.

*The Challenge*: Vasilisa must manage her fear and anxiety at not meeting the task requirements and risks death; instead, she completes the tasks with innate resources and courage.

*Reflections*: Going into the heart of a forest and meeting the Dark Mother are beyond terrifying.

This girl has the courage and heart to continue her journey and not turn back.

*Practice*: (1) What film heroines have gone through similar situations (e.g., the recent movies *Frozen*, *Tangled*, and *Brave*)? (2) What stories do you know where sorting and differentiation of tasks has occurred (e.g., Psyche and Eros, *Aschen-puttel* (Cinderella)—all having to sort seeds)? (3) For a few moments, think about a client who was courageous enough to meet head-on what they feared most. What did you admire in her?

## Center: Who Loves Us Best

*The Setup*: Who and what are we if we have no voice, if our life means nothing to others around us? Who nurtured our voice, our spirit? Who has loved us best? Do we count ourselves as one of those people?

*The Gift*: Our spirit is whole and shines even through the darkest of nights.

*The Challenge*: We forget to listen to the small, still voice inside our heart.

*Reflections*: (1) In the sacred space of the numinous, the self is nurtured and cherished. (2) As Vasilisa found, trusting in that innate sense of self, of intuition and discernment, most often brings us great internal rewards.

*Practice*: (1) Take a look at mandala forms: One lovely website is http://www.facebook.com/Sacred-Geometry-Mandalas-213593625344837/ or in books (e.g., Cunningham, 2010; or Fincher, 2010). (2) Create a free-form mandala yourself using colored markers or pencils and paper from your playroom. See if you can relate your drawing to the stage in the Great Round by working with one of the books by Susanne Fincher: *The Mini Mandala Coloring Book* (2014), or *The Mandala Workbook: A Creative Guide for Self-Exploration, Balance, and Well-Being* (2009), both published by Shambhala. (3) Take in these words from Estes, mindfully with your breath, about the Wild Mothers: "Usually everyone has at least one. If we are lucky, throughout a lifetime we will have several. You are usually grown or at least in your late adolescence by the time you meet them. They are vastly different from the too-good mother. The little wild mothers guide you, burst with pride over your accomplishments. They are critical of blockages around your creative, sensual, spiritual, and intellectual life. Their purpose is to help you, to care about your art, and to reattach you to the wishes instincts. They guide the restoration of the intuitive life. And they are thrilled when you make contact with the doll, proud when you find the Baba Yaga, and rejoicing when they see you coming back with the fiery skull held out before you" (1992, p. 113). Now, ask yourself: Who in my life has served as this Wild Mother?

## Gate 3: Holding up the Light of Truth

*The Setup*: The girl goes on the return journey and must hold up the light of truth, in spite of how heavy the burden, as well as look on as her stepmother and stepsisters are burned to ash.

*The Gift*: Discrimination of what is most important in that moment; the understanding that intuition is embedded in the very nature of our being.

*The Challenge*: To withstand the truth; to stand in the light and see the whole of life, of nature, of the cycle of life without judgment, with patience and clarity.

*Reflections*: Being able to bear the truth, to see with clarity, requires sacrifice and strength. Even the most innocent and youngest of girls must cross over to more complex, sophisticated understanding, because some traumatic life circumstances require fast maturation and quick thinking.

*Practice*: (1) Think of a client who is fearful of moving forward in therapy yet has demonstrated great courage in working through the tension of the opposites in therapy. What was the dynamic tension about for that girl? How did the she resolve the tension? (2) How might you, as her therapist, help her celebrate and solidify the quality of courage in her? Through words—creating a treasure box together—what wonderfully creative way can you both work to anchor her newfound ability? (3) Often, girls and women don't check in with their breath and bodies and emotions about the danger around and find it's too late, or have trouble setting healthy boundaries? Has this ever happened to you? Have you ever made the mistake of trying to please others too much, be too good, while negating your own needs, desires, health? Is there a time that you listened to that small inner voice of intuition? What was that like?

## Gate 4: Re-Turn: Finding the Way to a New Home

*The Setup*: This part of the journey signals the return to everyday life. In the story of Vasilisa, this would be burying the ashes of her stepmother and stepsisters and finding a home. In some versions of the story, Vasilisa is taught the skill of weaving by a wise woman while she lives with her father in a nearby village (i.e., the more precise details depend on whether the father is present at the end of the story, or whether he has died). This wise woman will guide Vasilisa to adulthood, in the way of a grandmother, a therapist, a beloved aunt, a loving friend of the family. In the continuation of the Vasilisa story, this wise woman takes the extraordinary weaving of her charge and brings the shirt to the attention of the Tsar. When asked who made the finest shirt he'd ever seen, he has Vasilisa brought to the palace, immediately sees her worth, and they marry.

*The Gift*: Rewards for a life full of internal growth, service, and the work of the hands in creating useful and beautifully made works.

*The Challenge*: Navigating with discernment to find the best mentor or teacher.

*Reflections*: Vasilisa chooses not to stay in grief and anger over her circumstances, but to begin anew, to find useful work with a passionate heart in apprenticing to advance her creativity and practical skills.

*Practice*: (1) Resilience can be the ability to navigate painful life experiences and challenges with either learned or innate optimism, or a combination of both, as well as a will to open the self to new experiences with flexibility and grace. In what way does one of your girl clients demonstrate this quality? (2) Using pipe cleaners, ribbon, wire thread, and cloth, construct a doll for yourself and maybe for a client, one just like Vasilisa carried. You can use the ribbon to wrap around the pipe cleaner, after making a cross with two of the pipe cleaners for the body, leaving enough on the top part of the cross to loop around in an oval for the head. You can then dress the doll, using the cloth and ribbons, and use the wire thread for hair, and colorful feathers to stick in the back of the dress. You can sew a pin backing on as well. As I tell the tale of Vasilisa to a girl, I begin making her a doll, asking her to choose colors and cloth, suggesting that she keep the doll for herself at the end of the storytelling.

## Consulted Sources

Aleksandr Afanasev and Alexander Alexeieff, *Russian Fairy Tales: The Pantheon Fairy Tale and Folktale Library* (New York: Pantheon Books, 1973), 439–47.

Clarissa Pinkola Estes, *Women Who Run with the Wolves: Myths and Stories of the Wild Woman Archetype* (New York: Ballantine Books, 1992), 70–110.

Marianne Mayer, *Baba Yaga and Vasilisa the Brave* (New York: HarperCollins, 1994).

www.soundstrue.com/store/theatre-of-the-imagination-volume-one-3635.html

~

# PART IV

# CHILD CASEWORK

*Utilizing the Journey Map in Individual Therapy:*
*Successful Reconnection and Healing*

To get to the simplicity of a thing, you have to go through the complexity, and only once you've gone into and through the complexity can you state the simplicity. What never rings true is the person who states the simplicity without understanding the complexity.

Susan Slater Blythe,
quoted in *Life's Companion* (1990, p. 264)

CHAPTER SEVEN

~

# Strategies for Utilizing
# the Sandplay Journey Map

In traditional Kalffian sandplay analysis of trays in consultation, as well as in many play therapy modalities using sandtray, the conversation and narrative around the creation of the trays by the client can become quite important when examining the dynamic symbolism within the choice of miniatures and finished trays. However, in selecting this case presentation for this book, it was vital to illustrate the Sandplay Journey Map gateways as clearly as possible. So we are not going to focus on what the client has said about the tray construction, but rather let the images of the individual trays "speak" for themselves through arranging them in gateways. This method of using the Sandplay Journey Map can be found on page 34. The form can be useful in several ways:

1.  *Strategy 1:* Clinicians would use the gateways in their "first pass" when looking over the trays, especially if the therapist is looking at the complete set of trays. This would take a rough form, so that they might arrive at a Sandplay Journey Map outline for use in later case consultation and tray interpretations. The clinician puts the numbered and dated trays within the gateways. Another possibility is that the clinician would take a tray or several trays during their work with the child and use the Sandplay Journey Map gateway descriptions to place the tray or trays within the appropriate gateway. In this process, the therapist can "drop into" the Sandplay Journey Map and gain perspective on where their client falls within the map when viewing one or two trays, within an entire process of trays. Clinicians can gain an understanding of where a single tray creation can be placed within the map after several initial sessions with the child—or even months of session work.

2.  *Strategy 2:* Clinicians would garner details about the clinical dynamics, symbol meanings, case notes, and history of the child's case and then use the Sandplay Journey Map to further gain perspective on the progress the child made over time throughout their treatment. This takes a rough form as well, with questions about

what is happening, and an outline of issues and possibilities for self-symbols and tracking elements throughout the journey process.

3. *Strategy 3*: Clinicians would first complete a thorough reading, analysis, and interpretation of all of the trays in succession, and then map the sandplay journey to present a polished picture of a completed sandplay process for later case write-up, group consultation, or case presentation. The Sandplay Journey Map would be presented verbally or in written form within the entire case analysis to individuals or groups in training, workshops, conferences, or publication.

One of the forms I use with sandplay trainees, the Sandplay Naming Sheet, asks the therapists to name the trays themselves, even when the client has given a name to the tray herself. This aids in helping the therapist more clearly understand the process of mapping the trays within the Sandplay Journey Map. For instance, I name the first tray "The Journey Begins," even though Lainey doesn't give a name to her creation. That helps me to see that a process has actually been started, because a path is clearly delineated, in addition to the tray containing aspects of a problem statement, resources, and elements (i.e., fire, water, earth, and wind). From the therapist's standpoint, giving their own name to the tray helps organize their own thoughts about the client and her journey. For instance, girls will often place horses or ponies in a tray. The tray name might be one of a competition or about the ponies having fun. I might call the tray "Gathering the Energies." The names of trays could be the same or ones that more closely correspond to "journeying" or "questing" language: "preparation," "gathering," "battling," "shadow," "tensions revealed," "integration," "harmony," or "return."

The following case presentations will follow two of the strategies outlined above, incorporating *Strategies 1 and 2*. Both Case A / Lainey and Case B / Jess will offer accompanying reflections about some of the symbolism and dynamics inherent in the tray progression when utilizing the second strategy. The decision to use these two less polished formats was made in order to assist clinicians to more comfortably use the map in everyday practice activities as part of the overall process of perspective-taking for case analysis and interpretation of dynamics and issues within the overall sandplay journey.

## Experiential Exercise: Outlining Case Presentation A Using the Sandplay Journey Map

Before turning to Case Presentation A's background information and journey mapping, challenge yourself to outline Lainey's tray journey without looking at the already mapped case.

1. First, take a moment to look over all of Lainey's Case Presentation trays—just the trays themselves, with no identifying information other than that Lainey is a girl of 6½ years of age.

2. Next, page to the Sandplay Journey Map: Tray Distribution Form found on page 34. Familiarize yourself with the map and the gates.

3. Try a guided visualization exercise. Settle yourself by breathing in slowly and deeply at least three times. Place yourself in a comfortable setting in your imagination, one with a pleasantly large, empty room. Imagine that you are standing in the middle of that room with all that space around you. Breathe in and out. Now, visualize Lainey's trays laid out in a circle around you on the floor. As you turn to look at the surrounding trays, the images of the trays begin to slowly circle around you and then separate into their respective gateways. You choose to face one way, in whatever direction seems right to you. As you look left, you see that some of the trays have arranged themselves in Gate 1. You look straight ahead, and more trays have arranged themselves into Gate 2; you look right and the trays in Gate 3 have settled into their places. You turn 180 degrees and there is at least one tray in Gate 4. Near to you, in the center, you find a number of trays are arrayed as well. Breathe in deeply again.

4. Try to outline Lainey's trays on the Sandplay Journey Map yourself below. What names for Lainey's trays do you come up with after you have arranged the trays in gateways? You may find that this naming aspect helps to crystallize your sense of tray identification within the appropriate gateways.

_____ Gate 1: Pathways: Choosing to Journey

Trays: _____

_____ Gate 2: Discernment: Facing Fear and Embodying Courage

Trays: _____

_____ Center: Illumination: Constellating the Self

Trays: _____

_____ Gate 3: Harmony: Reconciling Tensions and Integrating Shadow

Trays: _____

_____ Gate 4: Re-Turn: Appreciating Abundance

Trays: _____

# CHAPTER EIGHT

~

# Case Presentation A

## "A Journey to the Light" / Lainey

## Background

*Brief Background History:* Lainey was 6½ years old when she first created the trays, and 9 when she finished. Thus, we worked together for over two years. When her biological father found out he had a child, Lainey was already 4 years old and living part of the time with her maternal grandmother. Her father had a relationship with her biological mother, but was never told of Lainey's existence until the grandmother decided to contact him when Lainey was almost 4 years old. Lainey's grandmother was concerned over the neglect and sometimes physical abuse her granddaughter experienced. It was never clear whether Lainey was sexually abused. Her treatment in psychotherapy and later excellent adaptation to high school, graduate school, and social networks appears to dispute such a hypothesis. Lainey's mother didn't often have a place to live, and was in and out of substance-abuse programs and abusive relationships. Lainey's father had been married for several years before finding out about his child's circumstances. Lainey lived with her father and stepmother for over a year before I began to work with her in treatment. Her difficulties with behavioral regulation, school performance, and mood swings presented challenges for her parents. She developed a strong relationship with both her father and stepmother as well as with her younger stepbrother as time and the therapy progressed. Lainey used many play therapy modalities throughout the course of her psychotherapy; sandplay was the main expressive technique she utilized. She used the dollhouse, clay, engaged in ritual play with a snack before beginning the session's sandwork, played hiding games in the sand and the playroom, and made use of the many stories of brave children on the bookshelves, each of us taking turns reading to the other.

*Formulation of the Issues Facing Lainey's Adjustment and Healthy Adaptation to her New Family:* Lainey needed to work through her feelings of trauma over losing contact with her mother and experiencing neglect by her, as well as adjusting to a new family and believing that she belonged with them. As I stated when writing up a former child's case, the theme for Lainey is universal:

> the indestructibility of love and of the human spirit. Children are often brought to therapy when either they or their parents feel in crisis, in fear, with loss of confidence and self-care issues, manifesting in reactivity through stress, anger, and anxiety . . . [the] overall task was to face her fears of mother loss and abandonment and come once again to believe that she was deserving and capable of inner nurturance and love. "Finding the treasure within"—to recover the belief that love is inextinguishable, both as a gift to herself and a promise of hope—was our goal during therapy (Heiko, 2010, p. 174).

*Treatment Goals:* Therapeutic goals included establishing a healthy therapeutic alliance through providing a safe and sheltered therapy space and relationship; establishing self-regulation skills through mindfulness training; collaborating with both her parents and the school to work out an educational plan to help her fill in "gaps" in early learning; providing meaningful family therapy work every three to four weeks in the first year (and every quarter afterwards) for assistance in building healthy family connections and communications; and offering integrated play therapy treatment, including sandplay, clay work, expressive drawing, dollhouse play, and storytelling to increase her self-confidence and connect to her intuition and self-worth. Working with her pediatrician on care strategies was also a vital part of her overall treatment planning.

In using the Sandplay Journey Map, as Lainey follows her pathways, she begins to go in and out of the Center, especially when working in Gate 3. As a result of space considerations for this book's publication, the illustrations of trays in Lainey's process were limited to 20. There were 27 trays created in total by Lainey during her process. I do mention other trays she created in passing to elaborate on the themes and dynamics.

## Tray Distribution Form with Lainey's Trays: Strategy 1

We will first employ Strategy 1 (in rougher form, making a "first pass" to place trays within the gateways).

   __x__ Gate 1: Pathways: Choosing to Journey
Trays 1–5
   __x__ Gate 2: Discernment: Facing Fear and Embodying Courage
Trays 7–8, 10–12
   __x__ Center ("C"): Illumination: Constellating the Self
Trays 6, 9, 11b, 13–14, 18b, 19
   __x__ Gate 3: Harmony: Reconciling Tensions and Integrating Shadow
Trays 15–18
   __x__ Gate 4: Re-Turn: Appreciating Abundance
Tray 20

**Elements**

   <u>x</u> *Fire:* Trays 1 (standing fire and cooking fire) and 20 (lighthouse); 6 and 9 (lit candles and sparklers); 13–14 (lit candles and sparklers); 16 and 18 (sparklers); 17 (lighted candle); 19 (fire colors in the umbrellas/fans); 20 (lit windows in the lighthouse)

   <u>x</u> *Earth:* Trays 3 and 10 (mound); 12 (tiger standing on cave); 17 (island / drip mound)

   <u>x</u> *Water:* Wet Trays: 1, 3, 9, 14, 16, 18–20; Flooded Trays: 2, 15, 17; Trays with felt "water pond": 11–12

   <u>x</u> *Air:* Trays 6 (balloons) and 14 (balloons)

**One to Three Self-Symbol Representations (symbol name / Tray Number)**
   1. Drawing of apple tree with dark hole after Tray 7
   2. Both the little girl and boy figures in Trays 8 and 11
   3. One to several evergreen trees placed in Trays 1–2, 8, 11, 16, and 20

## Employing the Sandplay Journey Map: Strategy 2

We will now utilize Strategy 2 (garnering details about the clinical dynamics, symbol meanings, case notes, and history of the child's case and using the Sandplay Journey Map to further gain perspective on the progress the child made over time throughout treatment) for this case.

We can see that there are more questions about the process and symbolic movement earlier in the mapping than toward the end, as the pathways become clearer in the psyche's journey. Amplifying the case material by connecting fairy tales, legends, and myths to the symbols with which she chooses to work proves useful in gaining a more complete understanding of the case dynamics. Most of the trays in the Center require no name, since they are filled with metaphorical and symbolic "light." They contain a feeling of a numinous quality. They celebrate the "Treasure of the Light Within."

## Gate 1: Pathways: Choosing to Journey

*Tray 1 (Figure 8.1):* (wet) No tray name from child / "The Journey Begins" is my name for the tray. This wet tray is quite unusual for a first tray, even for a young child. Her descent into the sandwork is quick; she "digs right in" from the first moment in the sandplay room, without hesitation, after the first meeting session with her father and stepmother present.

*Details:* Girl setting out on canoe without a paddle, First Nations camp with teepees, and cooling fire and large open flames in the middle of the camp; fencing along the top right generally surrounding the camp, four evergreen trees, one small tree downed; bear, beaver, and rabbit families, one First Nations brave sighting his nocked arrow right at the girl in the canoe; medicine man dancing.

**Figure 8.1   Case A Tray 1**

*Reflections:* Setting out on a blocked path of water: Is this possibly a girl setting out on a journey toward the Self? Does her journey entail reconciling her water element with her fiery nature? There is a squirrel in the tree; is it getting some needed perspective? Does Lainey usually like to take stock of her environment? This could point toward good ego development. The scene is a First Nations village. There is a small cooking fire and a large, uncontained fire. The medicine man (is this a shaman figure?) is right in front of the fire: is he worshipping? preparing for battle? The fencing is not holding things in. There is a place where it's open to the wilderness around the camp. The rabbits (does this represent an aspect of the generative in the notion of Mother?), bears (could this represent the fierce aspect of Mother?), beavers, and downed rabbit near downed tree on the bottom right of the tray may represent family. The river appears to take the shape of an Egyptian ankh. The evergreen trees may represent a spiritual aspect. Is that warrior ready to shoot toward where maiden will go down the water path? There is a bridge present in this first tray, which is unusual: What is to be bridged? Possibly the instinctual energies and the more civilized but natural aspects of community?

*Issues:* Is the masculine overpowering the feminine aspect here? Is there the possibility of feminine wounding? Looks like strength and purpose abound; but there are many possible dangers. How can she negotiate protecting herself and still preserve adequate boundaries?

## Gate 2: Discernment: Facing Fear and Embodying Courage

*Trays 1b–1c:* Several trays in between the featured trays seem to tentatively explore the boundaries of sea and land. I name the trays "Moving Deeper on the Water Path." (There are no images of these trays.)

*Reflections:* Lainey spent most of her time getting the sand wet and creating space down to the blue of the trays. The red of the lighthouse cupola and the beach umbrella stand out. All the creatures in the sea are dolphins. (Are these representative of psychopomps—guardians and guides between land and sea?) The lighthouse shines light away from the rocks and gives perspective to the scenes. The palm trees provide spiritual connection and perspective. The First Nations women may represent the positive feminine; they look easy together but does that bonding appear possibly dangerous and unknown to Lainey? She made the women's clothing out of scraps and put a festive kite up for them. From the side, the tray looks like a feminine outline with her hair parted to one side.

*Issues:* These trays appear to represent the unconscious, feeling, early aspect of development. Lainey seems in touch with her playful side; and part of her is connected to the protective family. She appears to be appreciating a place of rest and peace, a creation of the opposites on land and sea. Is Lainey resting the psyche from the storms and upheavals she knows must come?

**Figure 8.2   Case A Tray 2**

*Tray 2 (Figure 8.2):* (flooded tray) No tray name from the child / I name the tray: "Perspective Taking."

*Details:* Five evergreens, ladder, two brooms, lookout tower, rock, fencing.

*Reflections:* Now all the trees are evergreens: One large one is down on its side. The ladder is down; it's hard to access the perspective-taking function this way. The two brooms may represent the feminine symbol of sweeping clean / cleaning house or also the darker feminine aspect of the witch. There is a tree behind the lookout tower. Is the tower a wooden representation of the tree? There is a circular movement to the tray. To the side of the rock is The Hulk, a man who has difficulty with anger and appropriate boundaries, which has been left in the clearing. There is open garden fencing, the angle focused toward her deepest self, the "hara" or belly energies.

*Issues:* Separating out feelings of abandonment, loneliness, fear, need for connection and strength, while wading into the deeper waters of the unconscious.

**Figure 8.3  Case A Tray 3**

*Tray 3 (Figure 8.3):* (second tray of the day, very wet) No tray name from the child / I name the tray: "The Mound Opening Up."

*Details:* Sand form.

*Reflections:* Does this mound possibly represent a volcano, or maybe a hole opening up in the mound of the mother's breast? This tray takes up a great amount of time (the whole session) and energy to open up, literally and metaphorically. Is the hole going down? Rising up from the depths?

**Figure 8.4   Case A Tray 4**

*Tray 4 (Figure 8.4):* (very wet tray) No tray name from the child / I name the tray: "The Accident"

*Details:* Construction barrier, rescue vehicles, cars, traffic light, mailbox, telephone booth, traffic signs, bench, motorcycles.

*Reflections:* Lainey has entered a sustained working phase. There is a large construction barrier, rescue vehicles, a car upside down. The vehicles are stuck in the mud. There is a white bench—again. Is this bench a place to rest and get needed perspective?

*Clay Work (no photo):* At the end of the session, Lainey wanted to make a butterfly called "Flutter." Does this speak to the transformative nature of the symbol, as there is some red (activated energy?) on the head and antennae? She names the butterfly "Flutter," and says "It will be able to fly everywhere!"

**Figure 8.5   Case A Tray 5**

*Tray 5 (Figure 8.5):* (wet) Lainey named this tray: "Lovely Pond."

*Details:* Three goldfish, flowering plants, beanbag frog.

*Reflections:* Lainey appears to be deep into her psyche. Does this tray represent what's below the accident in the previous tray, or could it be a response to that scene? There are fish swimming in the pond. Beautiful flowering plants are everywhere. Is she taking another rest in this tray, deepening refreshment time, showing the vulnerability of life at the pond's edge? The frog she put into the tray was originally given to my daughter during one of her hospitalizations and used for cuddling time for a while (then given to me by my daughter "for the kids" in the sandplay room). That use of the symbol could point toward a deepening of the co-transference between us as well. Frog is an animal that can mediate between land and sea, and is featured in the story of "The Golden Ball." In that tale, the princess doesn't want to reclaim the seemingly ugly, masculine aspect of the self but learns the hard way to honor her promises.

*Issues:* Many trays have some aspect of activated energies (fire colors); this tray appears to speak to the possibilities inherent in the transformative nature of animus (i.e., contra) energies, those energies that she might need to draw upon as she journeys.

## Center: Illumination: Constellating the Self

*Tray 6 (Figure 8.6):* (wet) This tray marks the beginning of the "Celebration of the Self" series of trays for Lainey.

*Details:* Man holding balloons, conjoined twins, farmer, children, white ninjas, ceremonial cup, candles, sparklers on wooden sticks, large painted fan in the back of the tray, colorful paper umbrellas and fans.

*Reflections:* Lainey makes a "Birthday Party Tray" here (Heiko, 2004). There is a man with balloons, a festive air to the tray; a farmer, children playing, the girl with her hand behind her head, and white ninjas. There is light here, in the form of the white warriors. Now we are back to fire in more bounded representation. Do the conjoined twins represent an as yet undifferentiated sense of dark and light in her psyche? There is a large ceremonial cup which she puts in the tray, and then lights a candle in it. The tray holds the feeling of sacred space. We both find ourselves holding our breath as we look over the tray at the end of the session.

**Figure 8.6   Case A Tray 6**

## Gate 2: Discernment: Facing Fear and Embodying Courage

*Tray 7 (Figure 8.7):* (wet, heavily packed-down sand) No name from the child / I call this tray "The Beginning of the Separation of Opposing Aspects."

*Details:* Fencing, horses, pig families, two trees.

**Figure 8.7   Case A Tray 7**

*Reflections:* This time the fencing and the boundaries of the sides of the tray are appropriately keeping the horses and pigs inside. Lainey works on organizing the animals. The pig families might represent the aspect of the fecund feminine nature; although sows have been known to roll over and crush their young if there are too many piglets competing for space with the sow. The horse energy here may serve to underscore the impulsive, emotional nature of the young feminine aspect. Lainey used a miniature pony from my childhood I had placed in the sand room. There was dark and light fencing. She seems to connect powerfully with nature, having first grown up in a city environment.

*Issues:* Continuing to discriminate, set boundaries, learn about order and balance, strengthening the co-transference relationship through the connection with the pony.

## Center: Illumination: Constellating the Self

*Drawing:* Self-symbol. (There is no image of this drawing.)

*Details:* Apple tree with dark hole, stars, sun.

*Reflections:* The tree with apples and the stars may be the manifestation of the formation of a stronger ego-self axis. Lainey spent the whole session drawing.

## Gate 2: Discernment: Facing Fear and Embodying Courage

*Tray 8 (Figure 8.8):* (wet) No name from the child / I call this tray: "The Little House in the Forest."

*Details:* Three evergreens, two autumn trees, house, little girl and boy, clusters of logs.

*Reflections:* Trees in the clearing around house; the little girl is next to the logs. Does she need fuel for fire / activation energy in the psyche? The trees other than the evergreens show they are getting ready for winter. In the story of Hansel and Gretel, the children are drawn to the fantasy gingerbread house and are caught by the witch. Here, the children find themselves in the clearing in front of the house. Is it safe to play there? To go in? Who lives there?

*Issues:* Continuing on the path into the woods with the masculine and feminine aspects of self.

*Clay Work:* (Same day.) (There is no image of this work.)

*Reflections:* Lainey wanted to make something out of clay and asked me if I wanted to make something with her. She picked a figure on the shelf and we each made the same symbol, a Mother figure of holding, arms encompassing middle space. Lainey's object proved difficult in terms of keeping the inner part together. She worked even

**Figure 8.8 Case A Tray 8**

though she clearly experienced intense frustration. When she looked longingly at mine, I silently held out my figure to her to take home as well as the one she created. That felt like just the right thing to do at that moment. Again, a moment of bonding occurred, strengthening the co-transference.

## Center: Illumination: Constellating the Self

*Tray 9 (Figure 8.9):* (wet)

*Details:* Ceramic red rose, sparklers on wooden sticks, candles, colored-paper roses, blue ceramic horses.

*Reflections:* These blue horses are more abstract than realistic ones from previous trays. The creation of this tray was experienced as very quietly spiritual, with the self-symbol of the red rose in the center of the tray, flowers, lit candles, and sparklers scattered all over.

*Next tray:* (dry) (There is no image of this tray.)

*Details:* Nine sparklers on wooden sticks, candles, colored-paper roses.

*Reflections:* This tray seems more centered and orderly, similar to Tray 7, earlier, with fenced-in farm animals. Lainey seems to be reconfiguring her neurobiological processing, seen in the squaring off of the miniatures in the abstract.

**Figure 8.9   Case A Tray 9**

## Gate 2: Discernment: *Facing Fear and Embodying Courage*

*Tray 10 (Figure 8.10)*: (dry)

*Details:* Pegasus made from rope, TV, and food in form of bread, cake, hamburger, pie, Cokes.

*Reflections:* The mound from Tray 3 has brought forth Pegasus, a horse that can fly!

Pegasus was foaled from a few drops of blood after Perseus cut off the head of the witch-goddess Medusa. In this tray, Pegasus has access to water, food, entertainment, and gains height (Is Lainey possibly reaching and attaining perspective from this height?) on the mound, facing left toward the inward journey. Is Lainey moving from the more "feeling" aspect to the tray associated with the mind, with logos? This was the first use of a dry tray, halfway through her process.

*Issue:* What does the free self (represented by the winged horse) need for sustenance?

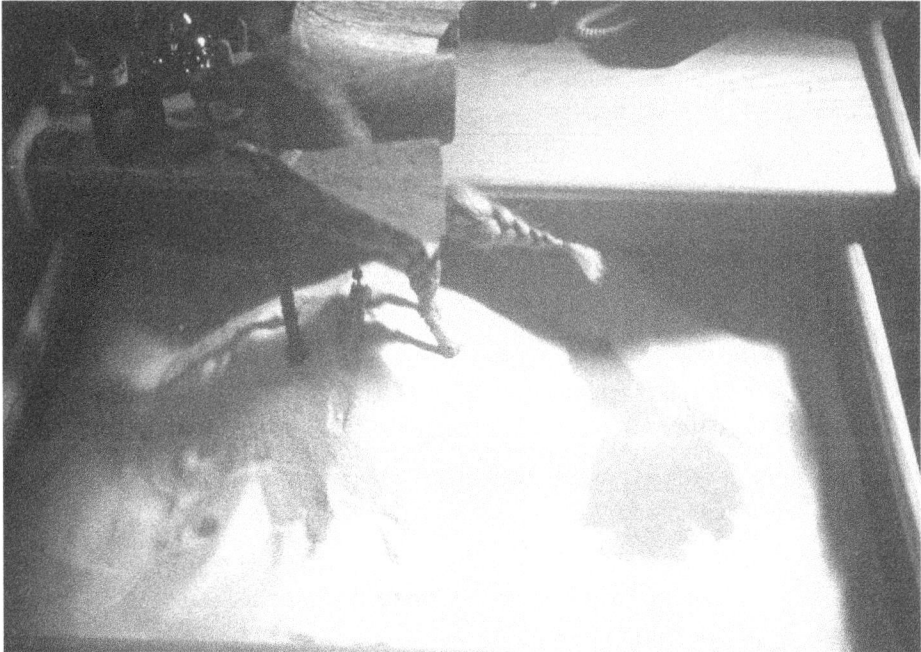

**Figure 8.10   Case A Tray 10**

*Tray 11 (Figure 8.11)*: (wet) No name from the child / I named this tray: "The Journey in the Clearing Continues."

*Details:* Two evergreens, two autumn trees, golden carriage, beach umbrella with two chairs, felt "pond," two Model T cars, pathway between the lake and the cottage in the mud, stone cottage. Inside the cottage, under the stone roof, boy and girl facing the food, presents, drink, little tiny evergreen.

**Figure 8.11   Case A Tray 11**

*Reflections:* It is still autumn time. The carriage moves from the pond to the cottage. Rest is available to the psyche in the cottage itself. She mixes the old-fashioned fairy tale carriage with the more "modernized" Model T cars. Inside the stone cottage, there is food, presents, drink, a tiny evergreen. The entire tray is more relativized from the previous Pegasus tray.

*Issues:* Lainey is continuing on the path and finding more sustenance in the form of resources as well as treasures.

## Center: Illumination: Constellating the Self

*Tray 11b:* (dry) Lainey calls this tray: "The Light." (There is no image of this tray.)

*Details:* 13 candles, which Lainey lit herself.

*Reflections:* This tray represents the continuation of the centering journey, with the sense of the numinous during its creation and our sitting quietly with it afterwards for the whole session in the darkness. (She asked me to turn off the playroom lights).

*Issues:* Demonstrating the simplicity and beauty of illumination in the psyche of a young child.

## Gate 2: Discernment: Facing Fear and Embodying Courage

*Tray 12 (Figure 8.12):* (wet) No name from the child / I named this tray: "Tension of the Opposites: Solar and Lunar / Lions and Tigers."

*Details:* All large animals: lion and lioness, giraffe family, elephant, tiger standing atop a cave, felt water pond, orangutan family, four groupings of trees more natural to a savannah environment.

*Reflections:* The water miniature in the center comes down in the symbolic representation of "yin," the shade or feminine aspect; here are big energies coming to the center of the tray, and two families diagonally opposite: the giraffe and orangutan families (the latter are among the most intelligent and solitary of apes). There is symmetry in the trees and animal groupings; the tiger is elevated on top of a cave. (Is this animal associated with "yang" or solar energies, gaining perspective?)

*Issues:* Facing Big Fears; and engagement with primal energies and the energies of spirit animals.

**Figure 8.12   Case A Tray 12**

## Center: Illumination: Constellating the Self

*Trays 13–14*

*Issues:* Showing the treasure and light within the self through using Isis and the story of her love for Horus, connecting by suggestion the animus aspect of her psyche.

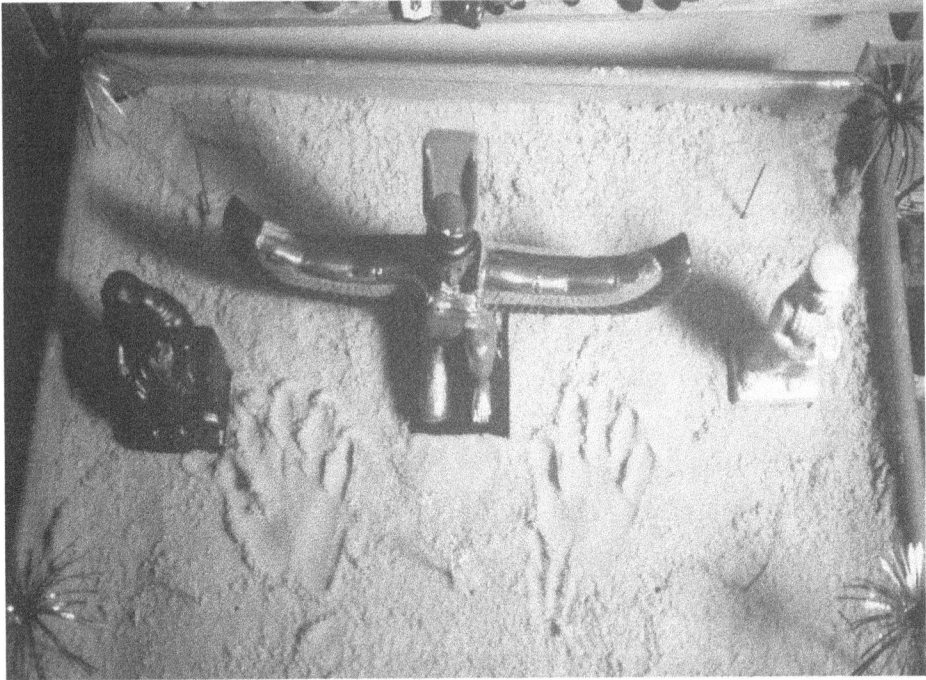

**Figure 8.13   Case A Tray 13**

*Tray 13 (Figure 8.13):* (dry) No name from the child / I name this tray: "Constellation of the Self: The Three Aspects of Mother."

*Details:* Six candles, Demeter, Isis, and Aphrodite, four sparklers on wooden sticks.

*Reflections:* Mourning Demeter, whose sadness at losing Persephone to Hades caused the earth to be plunged into winter; Goddess Isis, the great Mother; and Medusa, the menacing Gorgon who hated men are all represented in the tray. Medusa's blood foaled Pegasus in Tray 10. The four sparklers mark the tray's four corners. After sighing deeply, Lainey made the H'neini sign, "I am here," by carefully pressing her hands into the tray. The candles had burned down by that time.

*Tray 14 (Figure 8.14):* (wet) No name from child / I name this tray: "Isis the Great Mother."

*Details:* Balloons adorn each of the four corners of the tray; sparklers on wooden sticks, the Goddess Isis, adorned with jewels in the center; two masks embedded in

**Figure 8.14   Case A Tray 14**

the sand in front of Isis and two masks to either side of her, offerings of jewels to the goddess in a circle around her; candles, a magic wand to the left of Isis.

*Reflections:* Luminous, numinous: This tray sent both of us underneath the table, beneath a blanket that used to be my son's when he was little. We peered out at the Goddess, surrounded by treasure stones, a magic wand, candles, balloons, sparklers—in awe, and speechless for the rest of the session, smiling at each other and then at the light.

## Gate 3: Harmony: Reconciling Tensions and Integrating Shadow

*Tray 15 (Figure 8.15):* (flooded tray)

*Details:* Flowering plants, lookout tower, ladder, little green plant at the top of the tower near the ladder.

*Reflections:* Back to the watery depths: The flowering plants from Tray 5 have arisen through the mud (as the lotus flower does). This time, the lookout tower (first seen in a ladder-less state in Tray 2) with ladder attached is available for viewing perspective, with a spark of green life at the top.

*Issues:* Back deep in the "Swamp of the Tension of Being Overwhelmed," Lainey possibly experiences the fear that she might not get to enjoy the resources and connection she needs.

Figure 8.15    Case A Tray 15

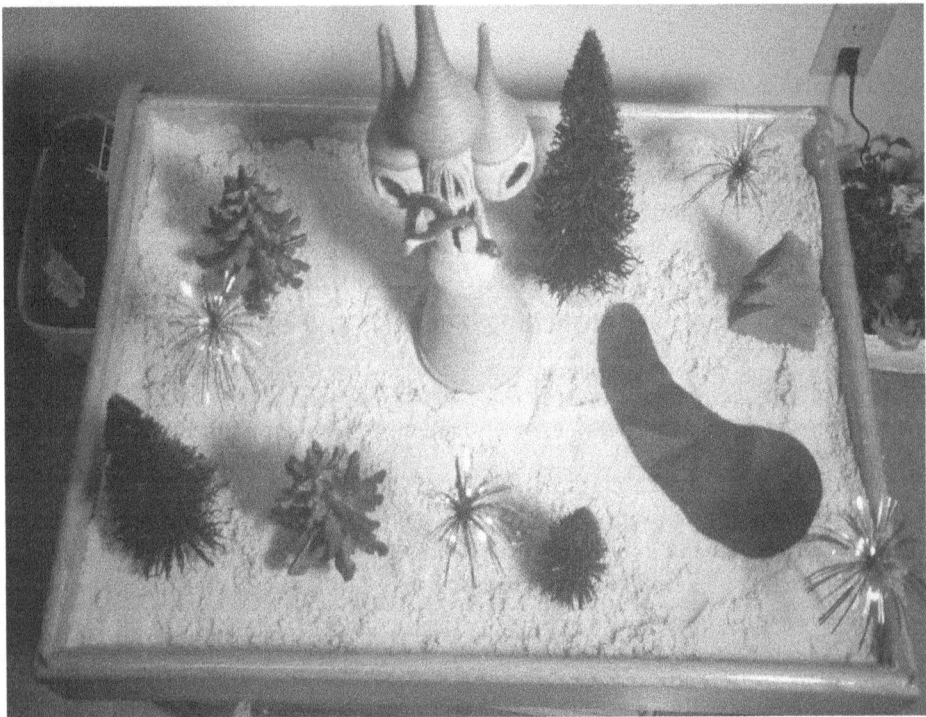

Figure 8.16    Case A Tray 16

*Tray 16 (Figure 8.16):* (wet, packed sand)

*Details:* Five evergreens, four sparklers, a castle, snake overlooking water. The snake prominently basks in one of the towers: feminine, with big energy, transformative, sensing.

*Reflections:* The castle is in the same spot as Pegasus, and before that, the mound. The large snake is curled in the tower bastion, its head looking toward the water, which has now moved back to the right side of the tray. This tray had the feeling of being watchful and protective in nature.

*Issues:* This is the castle of the king, occupied by the feminine (snake), which dominates the landscape, and is the organizing principle of "home."

**Figure 8.17   Case A Tray 17**

*Tray 17 (Figure 8.17):* (flooded tray) No name from the child / I name this tray: "Pilgrimage to the Sacred Mountain."

*Details:* Boats surrounding a mountain that Lainey created by dripping the wet sand on top of itself, drop by drop; three islands of mud hold a lighted candle on three sides of the tray.

*Reflections:* The ships from some of the earliest trays, about two years before the creation of this tray, now travel to and from the mountain, the place that had opened up its energy from Tray 3. There are three candles burning on three islands, and nine ships in total, her age at the time of making the tray. The mountainous island was laboriously created, drip by drip. She was very deep in her process here.

*Issues:* There is deep feeling of loss and hope in this tray; there is travel, commerce, light, and mobility available; but the depth of the unconscious goes through the islands where the candles burn. There is the experience of centering and an orderly, easeful feeling here as well.

**Figure 8.18   Case A Tray 18**

*Tray 18 (Figure 8.18):* (very wet)

*Details:* Four large sparklers on wooden sticks, two foam train tunnels, brass statue of the Goddess Kali Ma.

*Reflections:* Kali is the Hindu Dark Mother aspect of Parvati, Lord Shiva of Creation's consort. She may have sprung from the forehead in a manifestation of the anger of the Goddess Durga as she battled the demons. When Kali was thus birthed, she ate all the demons and strung their skulls around her neck. When she appears in many adult women's trays, I have learned to look out: Her manifestation almost always signals grand changes in subsequent behavior or life circumstances. With Lainey, the appearance of this Goddess, after Pegasus was placed in Tray 10, seems to follow a path of manifesting the Dark Mother energies of strength, vitality, and loyalty. The circular path around the tray leads through two tunnels, the place of darkness that comes out into the light. The sparklers delineate the tray at the corners.

*Issues:* Lainey possibly manifests the energy of Kali Ma as a symbol of transformation of her personal maternal internalization to a more satisfying and protective Mother aspect.

## Center: Illumination: Constellating the Self

*Tray 18b:* (dry) (There is no image of this tray.)

*Details:* Paper fans, cocktail fruits on sticks, small paper umbrellas; finger-walking pathways among the miniatures.

*Reflections:* Again, Lainey seems to make the journey to the place of calm, earth, silence, dance, and sun.

**Figure 8.19   Case A Tray 19**

*Tray 19 (Figure 8.19):* (wet)

*Details:* Paper fans, cocktail fruits on sticks, small paper umbrellas.

*Reflections:* Can Lainey continue to integrate the foreign aspect of the psyche (possibly the Asian fans) with centering and light (the fire colors inherent in the umbrellas and fans)? Here is order in the five rows, and light and integration in the abstract.

*Issues:* Lainey seems to be rendering a more abstract rendering of the grounding center of the self.

## Gate 4: Re-Turn: Appreciating Abundance

*Tray 20 (Figure 8.20):* (wet)

*Details:* Homes, mill, palace, Empire State Building, church, lighthouse, trees, people, haunted Halloween house, golden carriage, water path across the tray, stone bridge.

**Figure 8.20   Case A Tray 20**

*Reflections:* This tray represents a definite Return to the Collective. Lainey puts together fantasy and more regular homes: a mill, a palace, a lighthouse, trees, all relativized with small people among the homes going about their everyday lives, with adults and children living in harmony. In this tray, she appears to bridge both the scary places (i.e., the haunted Halloween house) and her fantasy life (i.e., the palace) of the unconscious with the more ordinary village life. The golden carriage, seen in Tray 11, brings the energy back to the hara center of its creator, from the collective.

This time the path of water goes across the tray horizontally, not vertically, as it did in Tray 1. The water path is continuous.

*Issues:* Lainey's tray showcases a triumphant return back on the water path to a relativized life in the "village/town," and integrates the dark and scary with the safe, strong places in the town center. Activity and industry mark this tray, with the horses fairly leaping to move across.

*Clay Work:* (There is no image of this work.)

*Reflections:* The heart within the heart . . . with healthy pink undertones marbled within the clay.

*Case Conclusion:* Lainey finished her process. Unlike many of the other children with whom I work, she never returned to therapy during any sensitive or critical times in her life. She continued to do well, ended up in graduate school, and has a loving relationship with her family and friends. Her stepmother has kept in touch with me over the years, to my delight.

When I think of Lainey, and her beautiful connection to the powerful protector Great Mother Kali, Verse 3.13.7 from the Chandogya Upanishad comes to mind, quoted in Olofsdotter (2007):

> There is a light that shines beyond
> all things on earth beyond us all
> beyond the heavens
> the highest heavens
> This is the light that shines in our Heart

CHAPTER NINE

~

# Case Presentation B

## *"A Journey to the World Tree and Back" / Jess*

## Background

*Brief Background History:* Jess worked in therapy for about four years, from about the age of 10 (in late elementary school) into early adolescence (into her first year of high school). Jess's parents were in the process of separating (and later divorcing) when Jess first came to see me. Jess's mother's goals for her were: "I want her to be her own person. She's not like other kids. I want her to listen to her [own] voice, she's got a different beat, and she's struggled with that. She doesn't collect the latest trends. She's lonely. She doesn't want to compromise herself." Jess spoke quietly and forcefully that "people always say talk about your feelings. I prefer to work things out by myself, pretend upsetting things never happened." Jess's mom reported that Jess disliked being treated "like a child," and often held her emotions from other children, distancing herself from them. Jess's mom wanted Jess to speak up more at school and church activities, to be more of an "advocate" for self-expression and needs.

Jess had a "hard year of tears" before entering therapy. She struggled with the hierarchy of girls bullying at school. In one instance, she was given an ultimatum by a group of girls in her private-school class: Be our friend and lose the friendship you have with a particular boy (the boy exhibited behaviors similar to those "on the spectrum" of autism, and Jess was his champion). Jess's response to this "girl drama" was often along the lines of, "If you're unhappy, why try to make other people unhappy?" She found most of the boys at school "very, very irritating." Jess experienced debilitating stomachaches before having to go see Dad. Although Jess and Mom kept a cat, Jess's dad refused to allow a pet at his home. Jess was helped by the interactions with the pet, finding the care and comfort of the cat quite calming.

Jess's father, with a military background, initially stated, "We're about civility," and that "I've laid down rules for her. If she slams her door, I'll take it off its hinges." My experience of Jess's dad was that although he loved Jess, he was a "traditionalist" and an authoritarian. He insisted things go a certain way by forcing situations with Jess to result in his self-interest. In my work with him on many separate occasions in parent consultation, I unsuccessfully tried to help him handle Jess's upset feelings. I urged him to give her time to "decompress" and spend time away from a fraught situation in order to process strong negative emotions. Being so sensitive, Jess was particularly upset by her father's dogmatic stances, shouting, and controlling behaviors. Her father would refuse to allow Jess to go upstairs and close her door; and would ask in front of Jess and her mom, "Does she still do that?" in relation to Jess's enuresis at night (in embarrassment, Jess would stuff her wet wadded up clothes in a corner of her room at her father's house).

Jess and Dad were both strong-minded, stubborn, often inflexible. Jess was the more open of the two in engagement with differing perspectives—politically, socially, and personally. In a session with a court-appointed parent coordinator in one of the mandated parent-child sessions, he demonstrated a great deal of painful emotion at being away from his family during one of Jess's early elementary school years. However, he was more focused upon how important his work was, rather than focusing on the loss his child experienced that year.

During the early part of the therapeutic process, Jess's maternal grandfather, who lived in another state, needed care from Jess's mom; he subsequently died. Jess felt forced to stay more nights with Dad. Because of his professional work schedule, he was disorganized, often bringing Jess late to appointments and getting her home to eat late at night (8:30 p.m. mealtimes), resulting in unfinished homework. Jess was a child who did not adapt easily to changes in routine.

Jess's father remarried quickly and with little notice, which affected Jess profoundly. The father and the new stepmother, who had other children from a previous marriage, were quite rigid in their parenting styles. Jess was an only child, and loved. Jess's mom was the most flexible of any in the family network and was quite sympathetic to Jess's needs and personality demands. If such a thing could be measured properly, Jess would fit in the extreme end of the introversion scale. Her need for alone time, quiet introspection, enthusiasms for internal fantasy play, and reading were anathema to her father and stepmother's plans for their newly assembled family unit. Jess did not see the need to accommodate her father's demands. She became overwhelmed and drained when subjected to noisy family outings and a household of extroverts. Two years after beginning therapy, Dad announced with little notice that he was remarrying and would seek shared custody rather than the more traditional custody situation where Jess would live primarily with Mom. He demanded that Jess be a "loving daughter" to the new stepmother, and tried to force his daughter to accept his new family, including step-siblings, all of whom were extroverts like the stepmother, a forceful and demanding presence on her own.

*Behavioral Observations*: Jess often didn't want to leave her sandplay tray creations. When feeling deep emotion, her eyes would redden, but she never cried openly. Jess enjoyed dressing in stylish ways, with boots and pants in particular (e.g., saying in an admiring tone, "I love how my black nail polish with silver sparkles in the light").

Jess often retold stories of cat warriors, based upon a book series she loved. These cats often sought peaceful solutions to problems, although this initially made them seem cowardly by other warrior clans. These cat warriors quietly and steadily built their new lives in her stories and trays. Jess was enthralled with the Tiffany Aching character in Terry Pratchett's book *Carpe Jugulum*. Tiffany was a trainee witch who grew from age 9 into her late teens into a "person who knows things" and a guardian/ protector figure with the ability to see "what is really there."

Jess exhibited a lovely sense of "dry wit" and humor. For example, upon taking up the figure of General Grievous (a scary *Star Wars* hunter and military man who used his many arms as weapons), Jess stated, "He'd make a really good piano player." She made up stories in the sandtray, verbally, and wrote many of them into a notebook. One story involved a brilliant, unaware girl who thinks that kids are "super spoiled" and believed that she should only go to school if she wanted to. She ran away to live in a bamboo house with lots of pets. (Bamboo can be quite hardy and can survive in most environments.) In another story, a girl of 10 was a half-mermaid, and with great confusion had to adjust to being human. There was also a beautiful island with different cities, each associated with different feelings. Jess dictated that "You can't leave the city" but could only exhibit the emotion associated with that city. In a story told during the seventh grade, a boy fell into a magic pool and, when splashed, turned into a girl.

Over time, Jess helped me to understand that s/he saw her/himself as gender fluid, and restyled the birth name with a more gender-neutral alternative. Interestingly, our conversations over and around the tray-making were distinctly separate from the symbols Jess chose to create in the trays. Jess worked almost exclusively in the sandtrays in the first three years of our work together.

*Formulation of the Issues Facing Jess's Constructive Adaptation to Family and Life Challenges*: Jess's work was to develop a stronger self-image and self-confidence; to assert the self constructively with the father; and to more fully attune to social networks and friends. Toward the latter part of the therapeutic process, Jess and I worked together to come up with "peaceful resolutions" for goals when meeting at the mandated sessions with Dad at the parent coordinator's office. Jess's resolutions concerned her perception that Dad and his wife were "trying to remake me" and she compiled a number of stated requests of Dad: "(1) Don't assume what I want (al- low me to say what I want). (2) Don't be an asshole to Mom. (Dad was frequently disrespectful and disparaging of Mom.) (3) Quiet doesn't mean I'm rude. (4) When you say, "This is your home"—my home will always be with my mom. (5) You think I can't manage my time, I need to tell you every subject's homework. I can manage my time."

*Treatment Goals*: Therapeutic goals included maintaining a comfortable co- transference relationship after the initial meetings, again through providing a safe and sheltered therapy space and relationship, as well as collaborating with her parents, her stepmother, and the school to better understand emotional needs and challenges. The sandplay tray process was completed during the first three years of therapy. Jess became irritable initially when I would ask if there was a name for the early trays; and I quickly stopped asking. We can see that although Jess's Sandplay Journey Map forms a trajectory forward through the gates, there is a return to centering again and again as Jess masters feelings and engages with integration of the tension of the opposites. Each of Jess's trays in this section were taken from the perspective of creating the tray, as were all of the trays shown in this book and in my practice. I have many versions of the trays that I take, which were not included here for space consideration reasons.

As we follow the Sandplay Journey Map, we see that Jess creates many centering trays. Although there were 47 completed trays over the first two years of therapy sessions, due to space considerations in the book's publication, the illustrations of trays in Jess's process were limited to 25. As stated in Lainey's case (Case A), these other trays are mentioned in passing to elaborate on the themes and dynamics. They are lettered (*1b, 1c,* etc.) to distinguish them from the trays with illustrations.

## Tray Distribution Form with Jess's Trays: Strategy 1

We will first employ Strategy 1 (in rougher form, making a "first pass" to place trays within the gateways). The Elements list presented below is by no means exhaustive.

___x___ Gate 1: Pathways: Choosing to Journey
Trays 1–4
___x___ Gate 2: Discernment: Facing Fear and Embodying Courage
Trays 5–12b, 14–20
___x___ Center ("C"): Illumination: Constellating the Self
Trays 12c, 13, 21–21b, 23
___x___ Gate 3: Harmony: Reconciling Tensions and Integrating Shadow
Trays 21c–22c
___x___ Gate 4: Re-Turn: Appreciating Abundance
Trays 23b–25

### Elements
___x___ *Fire:* Trays 5–6 (weapons, representing the possibility of firing them); 6c–7 (rings of fire and dragon canon); 11b (tanks, wood for fire); 15 (rings of fire, dragon canon, Phoenix, Firebird); 16 (Phoenix, fire); 17 (fire and paper dragons, representing the possibility of breathing fire); 1c and 18b (battery-operated candles); 20–20b (dragons); 21 (sparklers, paper dragons); 10 and 25 (the fire colors of autumn leaves)
___x___ *Earth:* Trays 1–1c, 3–4, and 14 (mountain); 18 (cave); 19 (treasure stones); 20 (Queen buried in sand); 21 and 25 (flowering plants); 21c (caves, foliage, stones); 22–22b (geodes, semiprecious stone trees); 24 (cemetery); 8–11, 16, and 25 (World Tree)
___x___ *Water:* Wet Trays: 1b, 3–5, 6b–6c, 10b, 14, 17; Flooded Tray: 9; Water represented by uncovering the blue paint at the bottom of the tray: Trays 20

and 24; Trays 2–2b (sea miniature); 9 (plastic pond); 9b (blue wooden rings representing water); 10c (small pool); 9c, 10d, 13, 21c, 22c, and 25 (waterfall); 11b (wells); 5 and 20 (small stream I made); 18 and 24 (Charon in boat)

__x__ Air: Trays 12, 12c, 15–16, 18, 18c, 20, 20b (creatures with wings, representing the possibility of flight: e.g., Archangel Michael, Phoenix, firebird, colorful birds, eagle, fairy, swan, white dragon with wings spread); 12b (fairy with pewter wings); 10 (tree with birds in nest or jeweled birds); 16 and 25 (tree with jeweled birds)

## One to Three Self-Symbol Representations (symbol name / Tray Number)

1. Princess Fiona: Trays 8, 9c, and 10b; several princesses in Tray 12, who possibly evolve into the White Queen: Trays 17 and 20
2. Twilight movie cruel vampire Victoria: Trays 8 and 10
3. Acacia "World Tree": Trays 9, 9c, 10, 10b, 11, 16, 25

## Employing the Sandplay Journey Map: Strategy 2

We will now utilize Strategy 2 (garnering details about the clinical dynamics, symbol meanings, case notes and history of the child's case, and using the Sandplay Journey Map to further gain perspective on the progress the child made over time throughout treatment) for this case.

## Gate 1: Pathways: Choosing to Journey

*Tray 1 (Figure 9.1):* (dry, same day as Tray 1b) I named this tray: "The World-Builder Surveys the Possibilities."

*Details:* Contains the glass jar on the right back; the small shovels, sand smoothers, and sweepers on the left back, dug down into the blue of the tray bottom.

*Reflections:* This tray, and the two next ones, appear to contemplate the possibilities inherent in this medium, from an engaged and thoughtfully focused client. There was a second tray Jess completed within the same day's session.

*Tray 1b:* (wet, second tray completed after *Tray 1*) I named this tray: "Readying the Ground." (There is no image of this tray.)

*Details:* very wet sand form in shape of flat island with blue bottom all around.

*Reflections:* Jess seems to be experimenting with dry and wet forms of the sand, preparing for what is to come.

*Tray 1c:* (dry, garnet sand) I named this tray: "More Possibilities." (There is no image of this tray.)

*Details:* The glass jar containing the sand implements is again emptied. The implements are now scattered fairly tightly in what has become the front of the tray, near

Figure 9.1    Case B Tray 1

Figure 9.2    Case B Tray 2

to the "hara" or belly center. Jess enjoyed swirling the sand to the blue bottom at the back of the tray in patterns and placed an unlit battery-operated candle in one of the blue areas at the top right section of the tray.

*Reflections*: More experimentation and investigation seems to be occurring with the third tray I make available to clients.

*Tray 2 (Figure 9.2)*: (dry) I named this tray: "Storm Coming."

*Details*: Blue swirling sea miniature, large dark rock miniature, pier with car on it, clipper ship and a pirate ship, the glass jar with sand implements inside of it, after using it to sweep the sand to the pirate ship.

*Tray 2b*: (garnet rocks) I named this tray: "Water Source." (There is no image of this tray.)

*Details*: Blue swirling sea miniature, acacia trees, two tigers (one orange striped and one white striped), a stream I had made with green sides, a large, dark rock miniature.

*Reflections*: Two ships are sailing out into the interior (left side of the tray) sea from the rocks, one a pirate ship, and the other a clipper. The sea is beginning to pick up in intensity. Is there a path for the pirate ship? The next tray used the garnet sand, and contained a blue swirling sea miniature, acacia trees, tigers—one orange striped and one white striped—and a stream I had made with green sides. The sea miniature and rocks form the sides of a triangular shape with the stream as the pointed (arrow) shape on top. Was this tray a close-up of where the sea begins, the source from the rocks? It looks like the savannah where the big cats, the solar energies, prowl.

*Tray 3 (Figure 9.3)*: (wet) I name this tray: "Reaching for the Mountain."

*Details*: Sand form of a mountain, tank, horse, canoe, sand sweeper implement.

*Reflections*: Jess worked diligently to form a strong base for the smooth mountain she spent the whole session creating. She placed a metal spike on top of the mountain and three means of strong warrior transport energies at its base: a tank, a sturdy horse, a canoe. But the canoe has no paddle (placed on a table), and the tank and canoe are clogged with sand, unusable. The horse's face is covered with sand as well.

*Tray 4 (Figure 9.4)*: (wet) I name this tray: "The Mountain Has Split into Three: Whose Side Are You On?"

*Details*: Soldiers in two different colored uniforms, pirate ship, buried sand sweeper implement.

*Reflections*: Here it looks like the large mountain has split into three small island areas. Soldiers possibly from two different factions combine to shoot at the pirate ship passing by from the earlier Tray 2b. The action is confusing, and unclear. It appears that some of the soldiers are shooting directly at Jess's hara (belly) center. The soldiers are behind fortified sand walls, but many of them are directly in the water. There

**Figure 9.3   Case B Tray 3**

**Figure 9.4   Case B Tray 4**

are many conflicting energies here, the marauders, the soldiers, the three islands (representing Mom, Dad and Jess her/himself?). Jess created this tray at an unusual angle, from the long side.

## Gate 2: Discernment: Facing Fear and Embodying Courage

*Tray 5 (Figure 9.5)*: (very wet) I name this tray: "H'neini."

*Details*: One soldier in green; scattered sand implements.

*Reflections*: Jess slid fingers into the tray, after mixing the sand with lots of water, making a statement of "owning" the tray by making handprints. This soldier's rifle is pointed outside the tray. The shovel at the right side of the tray points to the triangular form at the back right of the tray. Does the triangle represent the trinity? Some need for stability?

*Tray 6 (Figure 9.6)*: (dry) I name this tray: "Fierce and Dark Energies Emerge."

*Details*: Construction vehicles, people with cameras and video equipment, sand implements, two bridges (one broken down, with a big spider-like crack in it, and one with logs, covered with sand), Lady Vashj figure (from *World of Warcraft* video game: a highborn lady who was turned into a vengeful humanoid sea serpent) with weapons.

**Figure 9.5   Case B Tray 5**

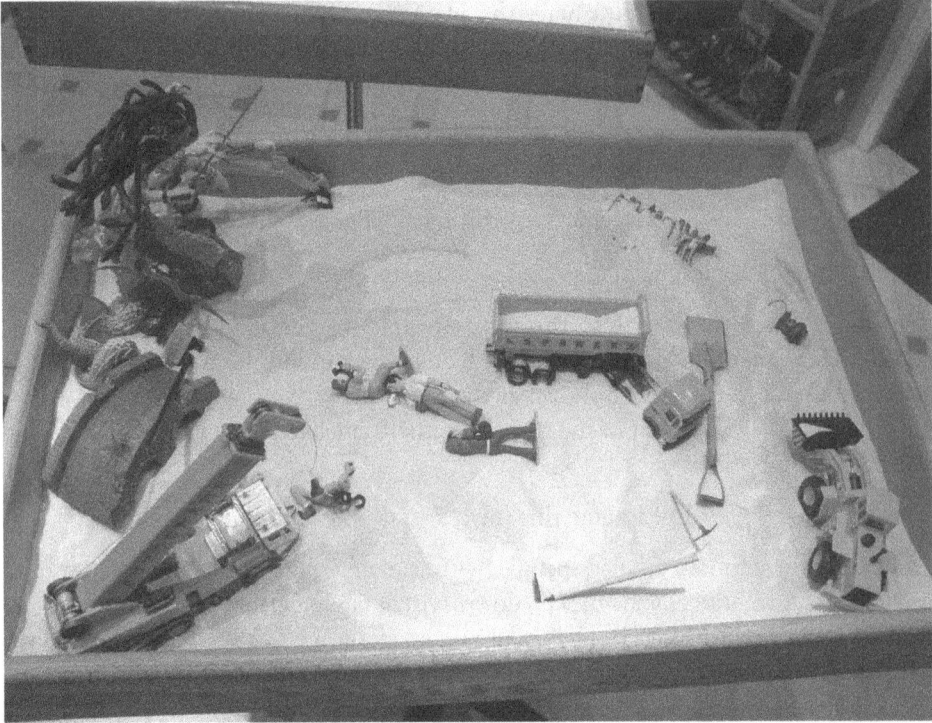

**Figure 9.6   Case B Tray 6**

*Reflections*: Right before coming to therapy, Jess received the news about a beloved grandfather dying. Darker energies emerge, in the aspect of Medusa, one of the Gorgons, whose visage could turn men to stone, and whose hair is composed of snakes, the strange bridge on the front left of the tray, and the fact that the two bridges in the tray don't connect yet to anything. The people with cameras are placed down in the sand, possibly recording what is near them? There is no clear understanding of what is being excavated.

*Tray 6b*: (wet) I name this tray: "Earthing." (There is no image of this tray.)

*Details*: Construction vehicles abound, and also a well, sand implements, and blue saran wrap, which was earlier used to make a small pond (it looks like the blue swirling sea miniature from Tray 2).

*Reflections*: Jess is back to demonstrating continuity in these trays, through the water motifs, and leaving the sand implements in the tray after its creation. There is evidence of a great stirring up of the sand, and the interior left part of the tray is open to figures, possibly later in the progression. If the well is for wishing, what might be the wish? If it is for more access to water, to the unconscious, can it be that instead of being flooded by conflicting feelings, Jess wants a more structured access?

*Tray 6c*: (lightly wet tray). I name this tray: "Vulnerability." (There is no image of this tray.)

*Details*: Fire representation in the form of detachable rings of fire, a dragon canon, a metal catapult, a guillotine, a sand excavator, one of the sand implements.

Reflections: Jess insisted on having one of the creator hands in the front left of the tray. There is a big built-up ridge in the middle right of the tray, and the two girls, twirling their skirts, appear unaware of the dangers surrounding them in the form of the rings of fire, and the guillotine, catapult, and dragon canon. There is a gap in the fire; but the ridge is steep. What is being excavated?

*Tray 7 (Figure 9.7)*: (dry) I name this tray: "Gathering Fire Energies: Wow, It's Hot!"

*Details*: Rings of fire, medieval decorated horse, dragon canon and projectile shot from it across the tray, sand implements scattered, guillotine, metal catapult, three candles in back left corner of tray (directly across from the triangle made in Tray 5), sand excavator, soldier in green seemingly aiming at the canon.

*Reflections*: Activation energies abound in the red and orange colors of fire, horse, projectile, and dark energies from the metal implements of war and death. There are

**Figure 9.7   Case B Tray 7**

three unlit candles in the tray. Is Jess spiritually connecting with grief and loss of the familial home, parental relationship, and the grandfather's death?

*Tray 8 (Figure 9.8):* (dry) I name this tray: "Moving to the New Land."

*Details:* Construction vehicles, roped-together boxes (one box marked "fragile"), dark vampire figure from *Twilight* movie, mortal heroine from *Twilight*, cats, Princess Fiona from the movie *Shrek*.

Reflections: This tray marks a passage to determine Jess's direction and choices from here on out: a marking of change from passivity and overwhelm to the strength of self-determination, in spite of fears of fragility. There is an integration of dark and light energies in the figures in this caravan. The strong heroine, Princess Fiona, from the movie *Shrek* nightly turns into an ogre after being cursed; and then after falling in love with the ogre Shrek, permanently chooses to be an ogre. She is extremely profi- cient in martial arts and problem solving, although she is embarrassed by her nightly shape-shifting. The tiger energy from Tray 2b has been channeled into the more tame (is a cat ever "tame"?) house cat, both light and dark in color.

*Tray 9 (Figure 9.9):* (flooded) I name this tray: "Prima Materia."

*Details:* Two acacia trees (one upended), stone bridges, tree branches, golden carriage, lots of buried colored stones, plastic pond.

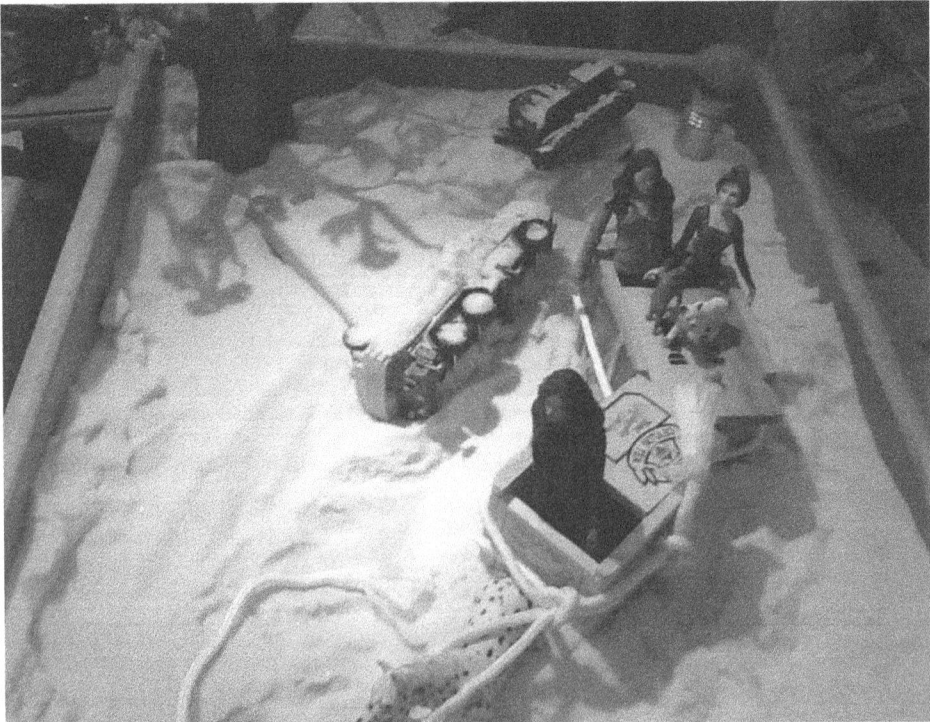

**Figure 9.8   Case B Tray 8**

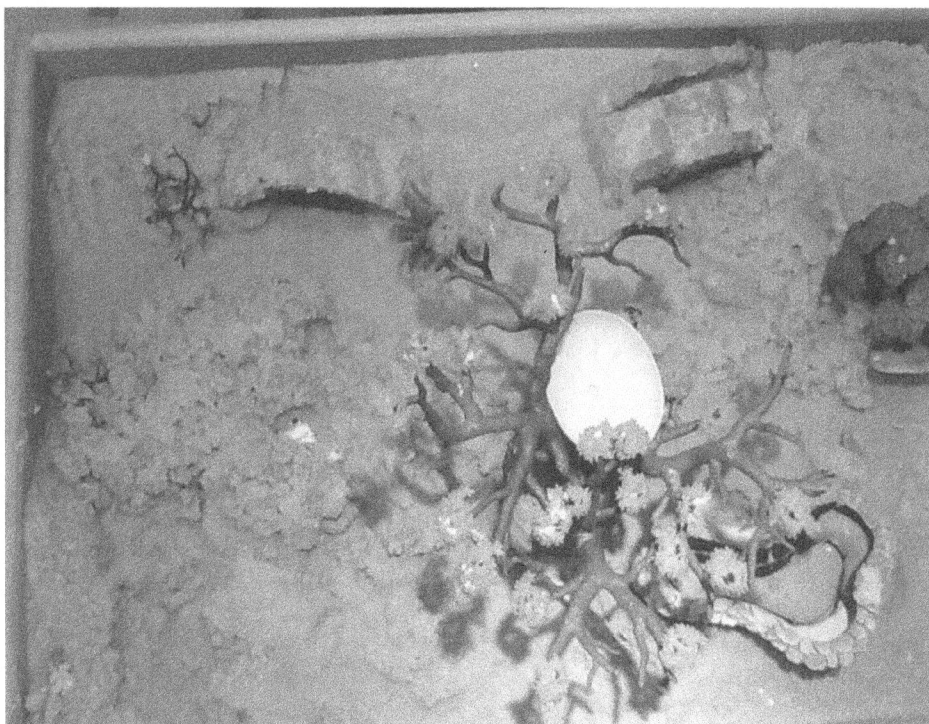

**Figure 9.9   Case B Tray 9**

*Reflections:* Is this the *axis mundi* or the World Tree in the center? This carriage has its roof upended in the tree, and the bridges don't as yet span anything. Everything is deeply churned into the mud, and the feeling of heaviness and the draining of energy was present in its creation.

*Tray 9b:* (dry) (There is no image of this tray.)

*Details:* Rocks, caves, blue wooden rings representing water, green leaves, hedges, soldiers, canoe, cats and mice abound.

*Reflections:* Jess puts her/himself back "up" in dry sand, at the "surface." Most children work with their tray progression in this way. "There is the going down; and the coming back up to breathe," reflected ISST teacher Adriana Mazzarella (personal communication). The rocks are scattered at the left side of the tray, some upended; and there are leaves all around, and hedges, as if there was a great storm. One soldier stands tall, looking out, the rest are mostly buried, except for their heads. Most of the cats on the right side of the tray are turned to look at the mice coming into the tray from the back left. The canoe, a means of transport, is upended and covered in sand.

*Tray 9c:* (dry) I name this tray: "Storing Needed Energy for What's to Come." (There is no image of this tray.)

*Details*: Open cage, Princess Fiona with sword, rocks, cave, waterfall, large acacia tree, greenery, stones, cats, parrot in tree.

*Reflections*: Princess Fiona rests under the trees with her sword at the ready, getting prepared for the storm of the battle to come. The parrot, with its gorgeous fiery energy, waits in the tree.

*Tray 10 (Figure 9.10)*: (dry) I name this tray: "The World Tree."

*Details*: Large acacia tree, flowering plants, leaves, stones, rocks, pine and palm trees; the sand brush is placed, handle downwards, in the sand.

*Reflections*: This may be one of the levels/realities in the mythology of the Cosmic Tree. This tree looks upended, but this may be another part of the reality the tree is in; or does it represent the upheaval in Jess's life? Victoria, one of the dark vampires, stands in the front left, looking over the tray. Interestingly (in addition to all the other wonderfully extraordinary things about this tray, about Jess's expression of the inner psyche), the *Star Wars* character of R2D2 is stuffed into one of the rock's crevasses. This resourceful figure, a robot that can repair and work with any computerized system, is unable to fix anything in such a position. Birds in their nests were carefully placed in the treetops.

**Figure 9.10   Case B Tray 10**

*Tray 10b*: (wet) I name this tray: "Up in the Boughs." (There is no image for this tray.)

*Details*: Acacia tree, rope and box marked "fragile," horses, cats, stones, Princess Fiona, sand implements.

*Reflections*: Here we might find the upper branches of the World Tree, with the box labeled "fragile" from *Tray 8* up in the boughs. The princess has moved to the other side of the tray, and stands waiting—but for what? The two horses seem to be silently communicating. There is excavating down to the blue of the bottom of the tray; the rest of the tray is dry.

*Tray 10c*: (dry) (There is no image for this tray.)

*Details*: Emperor from *Star Wars*, cave, rocks, treasure stones, trees, small water pool.

*Reflections*: In this tray filled with foliage and flowering plants, there is a small pool of water near Jess's hara center. There are some treasure stones on the front right; Jess created this tray with a long view from the short side of the tray. At the right back of the tray, the evil emperor in the *Star Wars* trilogy, Darth Sidious, lurks with arms outstretched. What can we make of the emperor showing up after R2D2 makes an appearance in Tray 10? Is the battle looming?

*Tray 10d*: (dry) I name this tray: "The Forces of Light Begin to Gather on Shore." (There is no image for this tray.)

*Details*: Canoes, *Star Wars* characters R2D2, C-3PO, Clone Troopers, waterfall, blue water crystals falling from the base of the waterfall, sand implements, hedges, palm and pine trees, large acacia trees, leaves, treasure stones in different colors.

*Reflections*: The forces of Light enter onto the shore, toward the forest. In the previous tray, we saw the emperor on the back right of the tray; it is as if this tray is an extension of that tray this next week. The treasure stones are massed in the forest area, possibly pointing to the vitality and beauty inherent in the earth.

*Tray 11 (Figure 9.11)*: (dry) I name this tray: "The Mystery."

*Details*: Large shell, gold-painted bricks, treasure stones, large and small acacia trees, wooden "jail," three pine trees, gold-painted pyramid, three pewter castles.

*Reflections*: There is a centering here, with the stones around the pyramid. Have the energies of triangle and the candles in the triangle shape from Trays 2b (the triangle between the three islands), 4, 5 (the triangle in one corner), and 10c (the triangle of shiny black stones) come together to create this symbol in the center of the tray? Treasures abound. The feminine aspect of shell, in its open position, appears to be a positive force here. Is there a jail for the dark forces, for the emperor?

*Tray 11b*: (dry) I name this tray: "Readiness." (There is no image for this tray.)

**Figure 9.11 Case B Tray 11**

*Details*: Two wells, tanks, large stone gate, two mobsters, barricades, police, wounded soldier being carried off, food, seedlings, wood for fire, soldiers.

*Reflections*: In this next tray, seedlings planted from earlier construction are watered by the Romanian well and the smaller well next to the patch. A chicken roasts on the spit. Jess insisted on holding the tray steady while I took the picture of the tray. A mobster, soldiers, tanks, and policemen guard this side of the tray, while the wounded are carried away. The woman mobster stands in front of the barred gate. Barriers enclose the scene as well. There is nothing on the other side of the tray. There is an atmosphere of powerful, watchful readiness here.

*Tray 12 (Figure 9.12)*: (dry) I name this tray: "Dark and Light Forces Align."

*Details*: Treasure stones, pewter miniatures, Tree Ent from *Lord of the Rings*, dark warrior, Dark Lord Sauron of *Lord of the Rings*, princess with elf warriors (both male and female) at each corner of the tray, two carriers per corner, stones, rocks.

*Reflections*: At the bottom of the World Tree, do we find the treasures of the worlds? They circle around the pewter figures, Charon in his boat, small castles, female warriors and sorceresses. Strong figures stand facing each other . . . one of them is a smallish princess in pink.

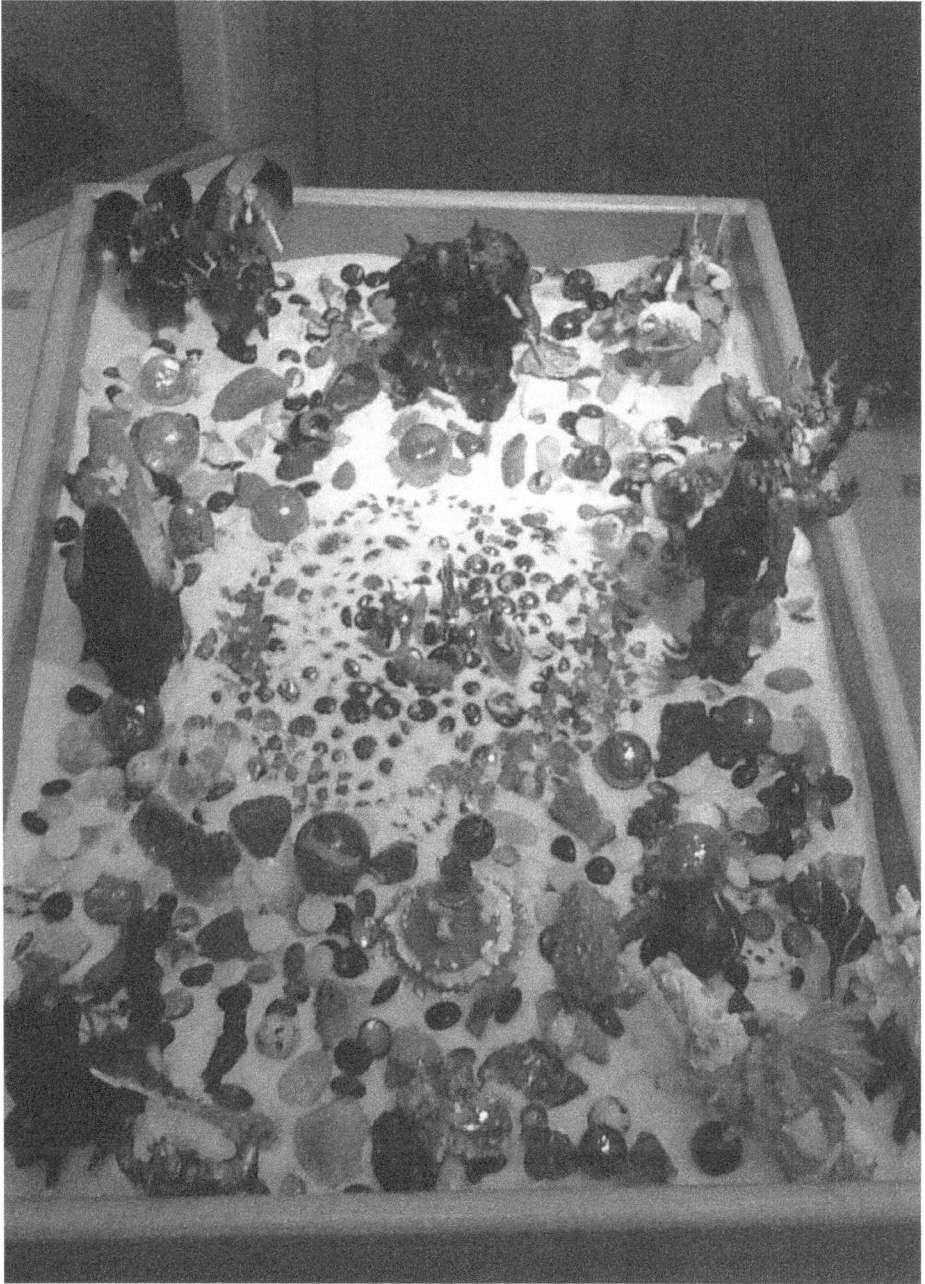

Figure 9.12   Case B Tray 12

*Tray 12b:* (dry) I name this tray: "After the Battle." (There is no image for this tray.)

*Details:* Treasure stones, semiprecious stones (amethyst, citrine), small construction vehicles, General Grievous from *Star Wars* stands facing the tray at the hara center, pewter eagle, fairy with pewter wings holding up a crystal, sand implements.

*Reflections:* This tray follows the face-off from the previous tray, as the world-builder opens up a scene of the aftermath of the battle among the rocks. There are treasures and sand implements scattered all over as well. The eagle at the back center and the fairy at the back right of the tray are left to stand against the general.

## Center: Illumination: Constellating the Self

*Tray 12c:* (dry) (There is no image for this tray.)

*Details:* Eagle, treasure stones, paper roses, large colored marbles.

*Reflections:* This appears to be a centering tray, with the eagle triumphant in the middle of the tray, and the energies swirling around. Have the dark forces been vanquished and absorbed?

*Tray 13 (Figure 9.13):* (dry)

**Figure 9.13   Case B Tray 13**

*Details*: Seven large marbles, seven cats, waterfall.

*Reflections*: This centering tray contains a middle blue marble surrounded by seven cats. There are seven colors of the rainbow, days in a week, notes in the diatonic sale, seven days of creation, seven being quite powerful. Cats were sacred to Diana, Goddess of the Moon.

## Gate 2: Discernment: Facing Fear and Embodying Courage

*Tray 14 (Figure 9.14)*: (very wet) I named this tray: "Scaling the Sacred Mountain."

*Details*: Sand form.

*Reflections*: This time the mountain is rougher, more organic in relation to the land-scape, with the blue of the water coming up to its base.

**Figure 9.14   Case B Tray 14**

*Tray 15 (Figure 9.15)*: (dry) "Double Phoenix."

*Details*: Forms and rings of fire, black stones and rocks, colored rocks, Pegasus, white alligator, a white lacy covering over one of the large white rocks, greenery and leaves, two Phoenixes, white dove with wings outspread.

Figure 9.15    Case B Tray 15

Figure 9.16    Case B Tray 16

*Reflections*: Here the colors of the triple goddess abound, circling the center stones. The two Phoenixes form a small line in front of a curve of fire, facing the central fires. Black, white, and red—the colors of the alchemic nigredo, albedo, and rubedo. Pegasus and the dove also face the central fire, on the front left and center of the tray, with Pegasus diagonally opposite the two Phoenixes.

*Tray 16 (Figure 9.16)*: (two trays completed, both dry, same day) I name this tray: "The Magnificent Land."

*Details*: First tray: Phoenix with trailing fire and peacock feathers; treasure stones; black stones at the far right side of the tray. The acacia tree hosts colorful jeweled birds, primarily red and white, clipped to the branches. Second tray: sand implements; the Oracle with golden disk stands in a clearing in an evergreen forest with the elf warriors from Tray 12.

*Reflections*: These trays were created together. In the nearest tray, we see the Phoenix with its "tail" of peacock feathers trailing behind in a beautiful spread, with treasure stones in an oval behind it. The Phoenix figure brings in elements of transformation and burning away the old to make way for new life, new possibilities. It is alternately possible that here the Phoenix symbol has become the aspect of the Firebird, the ultimate treasure sought in the heroic quest. The back tray seems to have the elf warriors, male and female, gathering to consult the Oracle; all are coming toward the structure. The creation of the tray had a numinous quality to it, with Jess smiling and lighthearted during its construction.

*Tray 17 (Figure 9.17)*: (wet in the first tray, dry garnet sand in the second; created at the same time, with only the picture of the garnet sand present) I name this tray: "Walking in the Land of the Dead."

*Details*: First tray: White Queen facing forward in the tray, front left; red ceramic rose on right front; pirate on guard, facing Jess's hara center; warriors facing the back of the tray; paper dragons on wooden sticks; Venetian millefiori paperweight; in the back of the tray are stones and fire, with the Joker figure in the center back of the tray. Second tray: Wonder Woman, Senex Superhero with trident, semiprecious stones in garnet tray.

*Reflections*: These trays were also created together. In the nearest tray, the Joker stands in the fires of what looks to be the Underworld, while the White Queen and her crystal (the paperweight), aided by her warriors and the Power of the Rose, stands to keep the worlds separate. The back tray, with its superheroes and treasures, also stands guard to protect the treasure stones.

*Tray 18 (Figure 9.18)*: (dry garnet sand) "Stones Stand in the Liminal Space."

*Details*: Cave, dark stones, semiprecious minerals, pewter Charon, brown bear, pewter Archangel Michael with sword, white swan.

Figure 9.17    Case B Tray 17

**Figure 9.18   Case B Tray 18**

*Reflections*: The tray was created from this short side, with the long side providing perspective. There is Charon in his boat, facing in the direction of Jess's hara center. Is it possible he rows to pick up a new soul to bring back over the crossing to the Underworld? The immutable quality of stone is apparent in this tray. There is one white standing stone placed in the center of the tray. Bear (dark) and Swan (light) aspects of the guardians face each other in the center, with Archangel Michael raising his sword in a gesture of protection? As the defender? It is highly possible that this is the continuation of the previous garnet sandtray with the stones and superheroes. For who can stand against an archangel?

*Tray 18b*: (dry) I name this tray: "Vigilance at the Forest Floor." (There is no image for this tray.)

*Details*: Battery-operated candles, flowers, plants, leaves, Batman.

*Reflections*: Batman stands in the center of the tray, facing the left side. The candles are flickering among the foliage. Batman's parents were murdered when he was a child; and the Caped Crusader, the Dark Knight as he is also called, is a vigilante. One of his major foes is the Joker from Tray 17, his nemesis, who also fought Wonder Woman in the comics.

*Tray 18c*: (dry) (There is no image for this tray.)

**Figure 9.19   Case B Tray 19**

*Details*: Jeweled birds, colorful stones.

*Reflections*: The multihued abstract of this tray echoes the color and energy of the previous tray. Jess operates in the world by reflecting on others' verbalizations and behaviors. She clearly enjoys the "crystallization" of these concepts.

*Tray 19 (Figure 9.19)*: (dry) I name this tray: "Meeting at the Crossroads."

*Details*: Four elf warriors on horses (two male, two female); multicolored stones in white, blue, and black; green marbles in the front of the tray.

*Reflections*: This tray is crossed in the center by the white stones. The Elves face each other on their quadrant of stones. Perhaps the Oracle from Tray 16 spoke of a future meeting of like minds and hearts?

*Tray 20 (Figure 9.20)*: (dry) I name this tray: "Sharing That We Know the Name of Everything."

*Details*: Ring of stones, island ringed by the blue of the bottom of the tray, white dragon with wings spread, stream, White Queen buried to her waist in sand, gray dragon with wings spread.

*Reflections*: The ring of stones, set on an island in a sea, speaks to the grounding of the two dragons and the White Queen, sinking their energy into the sand, almost

**Figure 9.20   Case B Tray 20**

dissolving their potential fire and strength directly into the earth. The right back of the tray in the water with its black stones, is mirrored by sand forms on the opposite side of the tray. The stream on the right of the tray, further bounds the ring of stones around the center figures.

*Tray 20b*: (dry, same day) I name this tray: "Flourishing." (There is no image for this tray.)

*Details*: Two dragons, White Queen, flowers, plants.

*Reflection*: Jess covered the two dragons and White Queen with a bouquet of flowering plants and roses.

## Center: Illumination: Constellating the Self

*Tray 21 (Figure 9.21)*: (dry) I name this tray: "Celebrating the Light and Beauty of the Self."

*Details*: Peacock feathers, sparklers on wooden sticks, paper dragons, fans, colorful paper roses.

**Figure 9.21   Case B Tray 21**

*Reflections*: Jess stood up the peacock feathers, and sparklers, paper dragons, fans, and paper roses all decorated this gorgeously colored and joyous tray. Eyes sparkling, Jess's mood was festive. When the tray was finished, a deep quiet had formed between us.

*Tray 21b*: (wet) I name this tray: "Here We Share the Treasure in the Psyche." (There is no image for this tray.)

*Details*: Colored gems, marbles, stones, tiles, semiprecious rocks, gold-painted bricks, large marbles.

*Reflections*: Here we can find the unique, the mundane, the treasures of the self in all their sparkling, matte, ordinary, and extraordinary glory. Each has a section, each is accorded space.

## Gate 3: Harmony: Reconciling Tensions and Integrating Shadow

*Tray 21c*: (two trays completed, dry and wet, same day) I name this tray: "Amplification." (There is no image for this tray.)

*Details*: First tray: colored marbles; Second tray: streams, waterfalls, abundance of flowering plants, leaves and foliage, caves, hedges, stones.

*Reflections*: The treasures from the previous tray have been shared in the back tray in abundance in the landscape; and in the front tray in the abstract, echoing the brilliant colors of the tray with foliage.

*Tray 21d*: (dry) I name this tray: "Flow." (There is no image for this tray.)

*Details*: Riverbed sections, rocks, colored stones, marbles.

*Reflections*: This can be seen as a detail of the previous tray, the stream underneath and among all the flowers and plants.

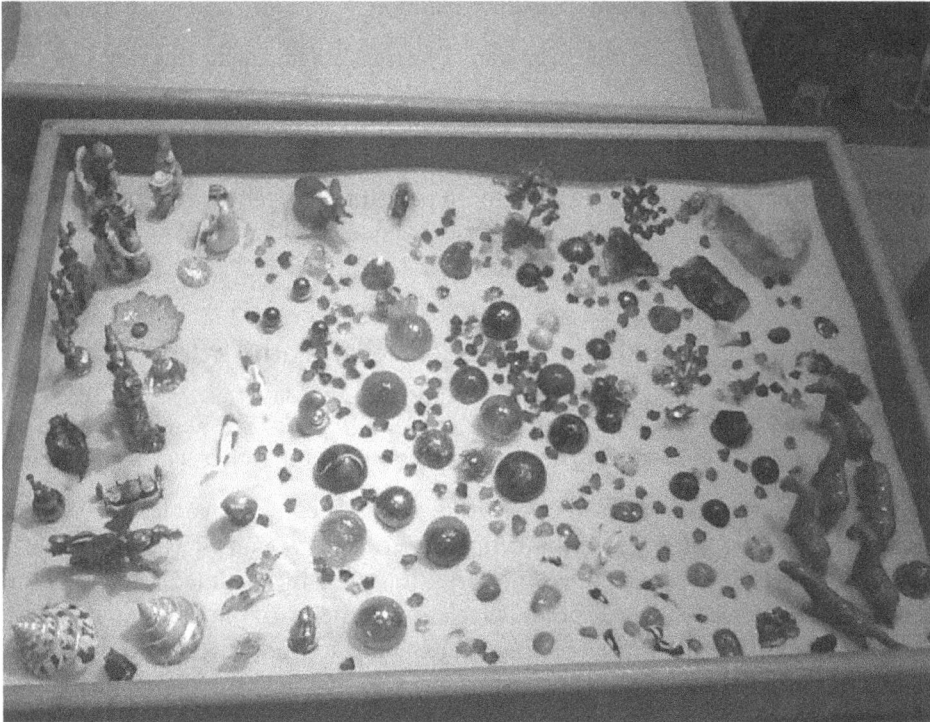

**Figure 9.22   Case B Tray 22**

*Tray 22 (Figure 9.22)*: (dry) I name this tray: "Diana's Arrow."

*Details*: Pewter treasures in the form of miniature castles with crystals, a fairy on a boat, exquisite ceramic miniatures, a red treasure stone on top of a leaf bowl, large marbles, shells, a brass elephant, semiprecious stone trees, rocks, colored treasure stones, geodes, blue ceramic horses.

*Reflections*: The Guardians of this sacred place stand at the corners of the tray: geodes, ceramic horses and figures, shells. In the center can be found a triangular arrow shape of the large colored marbles, with the Madonna and Child at the base, the arrow facing toward the right side of the tray. The bases of the semiprecious trees mirror the arrow shape. Have the symbolic triangular shapes in Trays 2b, 4, 5, and 10d all come together to form Diana's Arrow in this tray? Waldorf Education celebrates archery for children to target "a thought with precision, power and poignancy—and as true as an arrow" (McMillan, 2015).

*Tray 22b:* (dry) (There is no image for this tray.)

*Details:* Ceramic red rose, flowering plants, foliage, geodes, semiprecious stones, small stones.

*Reflections:* Here we can find the treasures of and on the earth in abundance once again, laid out in an inviting and organized fashion.

*Tray 22c:* (dry) I name this tray: "Habitat." (There is no image for this tray.)

*Details:* Homes and buildings, a painted Asian screen with natural scenes, a waterfall, a large acacia tree, castle blocks.

*Reflections:* Acacia trees are also called thorn or point trees. The scene shows fantasy and real palaces, homes and buildings in cities bounded by greenery. The castle blocks may represent the ruins of older civilizations.

## Center: Illumination: Constellating the Self

*Tray 23 (Figure 9.23):* (dry) constellation of the self tray.

*Details:* Large colored marbles, concentric circles of treasure stones, paper roses.

*Reflections:* This tray is composed of exquisite spirals of colorful marbles, treasures of labradorite circling the Venetian millefiori paperweight I brought back from highschool travels to Italy. (Sometimes it's useful to note which miniatures come from special places, moments, or collections in relation to the co-transference. In this case, this special paperweight is the metaphorical amplification of treasure brought back from a special trip I took; this is the second time Jess has used this paperweight.)

## Gate 4: Re-Turn: Appreciating Abundance

*Tray 23b:* (dry) I named this tray: "Rising." (There is no image for this tray.)

*Details:* Ladders, columns, staircases, doorways, labyrinth stone, open treasure chest, small pyramid crystals, globes (one encased in acrylic).

*Reflections:* Putting these ladders into the tray, attempting to scale the heights—does this represent the connection between the spiritual and earthly realms? With Yggdrasil, the Norse World Tree, the *axis mundi* moves up and down through these planes. Or is it the desire to climb to reach the metaphysical, that aspect which mediates (and brings together) between body, heart, mind, and spirit in the psyche?

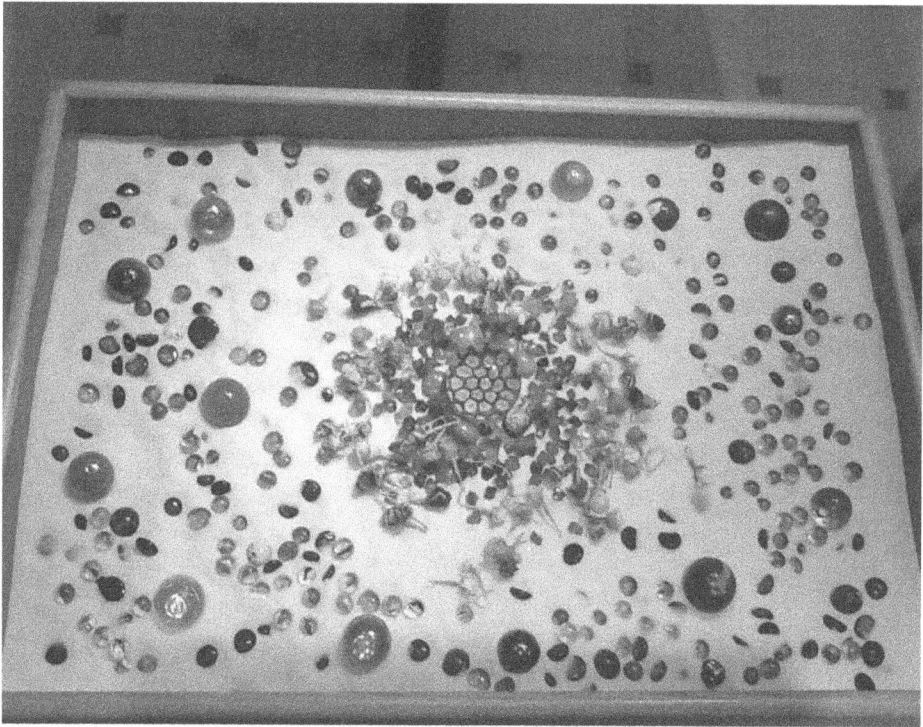

**Figure 9.23   Case B Tray 23**

*Tray 24 (Figure 9.24)*: (dry) I name this tray: "Quiet in the Soul."

*Details*: Water and earth, cemetery bounded by bricks with three entrances to three sand-covered bridges, castles on the side of the tray, Charon in the boat, gravestones.

*Reflections*: After the "ascension" from the previous tray, we find the "coming down to earth" of the present tray. This cemetery is a place of rest, of serenity in the quiet. What was stirred up in conflict, darkness, and strife through the construction trays has now been buried safely. Those emotions and experiences—in this spiral of the great round—has found peace.

*Tray 25 (Figure 9.25)*: (dry) I name this tray: "Back Again."

*Details*: Colored treasure stones, paper roses, foliage, flowering plants, large acacia tree with jeweled birds attached, waterfall.

*Reflections*: The World Tree, covered with sparkling birds and circled with blue stones and treasures, offers refreshment in its shade and dazzling beauty. This tree represents the flourishing psyche, connected from deep internal grounding to the spiritual aspect—and is a full journey away in the Sandplay Journey Map cycle from

**Figure 9.24   Case B Tray 24**

**Figure 9.25   Case B Tray 25**

the upended tree we discovered in Tray 10. All is present in this tray: the elements of earth, air, fire, and water in symbolic and literal representation. This is the juicy treasure to be found in the psyche. Jess has integrated vital family experiences and synthesized the idea that it is necessary to have shadow for the light to exist . . . and they can coexist in harmonious diversity.

*Discussion:* There were a number of aspects that conveyed the expression of gender fluidity throughout Jess's sandplay and play therapy work.

a. Jess frequently worked with both the wet and dry trays on the same day. This can be seen as an expression of the comfort with dual nature throughout the sandplay process (e.g., in Trays 1a and 1b, 2a and 2b, 16a and 16b, 17a and 17 b, 20a and 20b, and 21c and 21d). With some children, working with so many trays at once (sometimes Jess worked with three trays in one session) could be viewed as the child expressing difficulty with containing bigger emotions and "spilling over" from tray to tray. Jess's trays were created deliberately and with intention, enlarging and precisely engaging with the characters and amplifying aspects of her sandplay stories.

b. Back on pages 37–38, reference was made to boys' trays being rougher, messier, and containing battle after battle. In these rougher, unfinished, raw battle trays, boys make minute adjustments over and over, week after week, between two forces. As we view the progression of Jess's trays, we can see the use of soldiers in the middle of Jess's process, different from the more "feminine" symbols of princesses, fairies, and enchanted kingdoms more typically seen in girls' trays (although Jess includes these more traditionally feminine figures as well). Jess divides trays with gullies between the opposing forces and burying the fighting soldiers—similar to more "masculine" trays created by boys. An airplane crashes into a mountain, cracking the asphalt on its runway, missiles are fired into a sand "fence," "bullets" are shot at soldiers, a warrior claims the top of an excavated mountain, fierce sandstorms are created by delicate fans over the sand in strongly "masculine" pathways.

c. Jess is comfortable using construction vehicles in many of the earlier trays, digging, mounding, grabbing, pulling, sawing, burying, and scooping the sand. This is more typical of actions in trays created by boys. Jess covers and scoops sand, hitting and squeezing the sand into balls using chopping and hard squeezes. Interestingly, at times Jess also stirs the sand as if stirring food, something that is a more "typical" girl practice with pretend food preparation play activities.

d. One time Jess blew so hard into one mound that spittle flew into it. Jess didn't apologize or say "sorry" as many girls would do when that happened; she just accepted that was what she wanted and needed to do. Jess felt empowered as a full being in the playroom, able to articulate feelings (i.e., saying, "I'm doing just what I feel like doing" spontaneously during one of the sessions) and act without judging the self. "I know I'm making a huge mess here," Jess said right after creating three trays at once, after her grandfather died. No further explanation or apology was needed, as we exchanged glances. "So it is," I said. Another time, Jess mused, "It's fun to destroy things; why is that?" while placing a tree (the World Tree?) upside down into one of the trays. There was little hesitancy in Jess's motions; Jess created confidently, with surety—claiming the space. That would seem to encompass gender neutral behavior, in its best aspect.

*Case Conclusion:* Jess used many symbols of archetypal warrior energies in the trays, and engaged with animus and anima aspects of the self in a clear integration of light and dark, masculine and feminine, strength and nurturance. Using the self-symbol of Fiona from the movie *Shrek,* as well as the Amazon Wonder Woman, combined the aspects of the warrior goddess with the compassionate heart this child bears. There was abundance and sustenance in the gorgeously flowering and colored treasures of the trays. Like the Phoenix, Jess reinvented the self in a more balanced and nuanced way.

Over time, Jess found more and more friends within the circle of girls in her school and within the social hierarchy. She looked for the unique and the outsiders more often than not, but fit in well with almost everyone. Jess and Mom read *Queen Bees and Wannabes* (Wiseman, 2016) together, at my suggestion, early on in therapy. Jess came in laughing one time, saying one of the "best parts" of the book was that "I like how the mom [in the book] says, 'My darling would NEVER act like that'—listen up, parents, and *pay attention*! They do!"

Jess continued to celebrate strengths and the connection shared with family and friends. Her relationship with her stepmother improved and included many planned clothing shopping trips. Jess tried hard to find points of mutual interest and engagement with Dad, enjoying stories of his early years and similar humor. Even though Jess was clearly a "cat" person, there was a joyful engagement with my dog in the latter part of the therapy process, whereby Jess demonstrated patience and a sweet response to the puppy's antics. The sense of gender fluidity and inclusiveness as a human being, present throughout the latter part of her therapy work, connected her to a wider circle of friendships within her private-school program and with new relationships made through progressive church activities and social media.

If any quote could sum up Jess's life perspective, it would be this one:

"Because that was the point, wasn't it? You had to *choose.* You might be right, you might be wrong, but you had to choose, knowing that the rightness or wrongness might never be clear or even that you were deciding between two sorts of wrong, that there was no *right* anywhere. And always, *always,* you did it by yourself. You were the one there, on the edge, watching and listening. Never any tears, never any apology, never any regrets . . . . You saved all that up in a way that could be used when needed" (Pratchett, 2009).

~

# PART V

# SYNERGY

## Consulting about the Sandplay Journey Map with Colleagues and Mentors

Let the beauty we love be what we do.

Rumi, "A Great Wagon"
Translated by Coleman Barks
Reprinted with permission

# CHAPTER TEN

~

# Employing the Sandplay Journey Map in Consultation and Case Write-Ups

## Clinical Strategies

Consulting with professionals, or supervising them through a legal contract, can bring issues of adequacy and worthiness front and center with trainees. This relationship can bring out the best in each of the participants and also highlight some of the unresolved professional issues with which both are navigating. "At the heart of supervision is a focus on the supervisee's feelings, reactions, thoughts, and fantasies that emerge as a result of his or her relationship to the client and to the entire clinical matrix. The task of the supervisor is to bring all of his or her cognitive knowledge, experience, feeling and intuitive capacities, and communication and relational skills, along with a generosity of spirit, to the supervision sessions" (Friedman & Mitchell, 1994, p. 3).

The Sandplay Journey Map has become a means to develop therapists' understanding of the process underlying the progression of sandtrays from beginning to wherever the client finishes in that cycle of a piece of their work in sand. Therapists participating in individual or group consultation are asked to reflect upon and then fill out a number of forms before completing the Sandplay Journey Map protocol. Therapists who begin working with me in consultation and training are given two protocols with which to begin working in sessions:

a. Tray Description: This includes a diagram of the tray for the therapist to sketch out object placement and movement; which miniatures were used and in which order for later recall and analysis/processing.

b. VERDO Sandplay Session Evaluation: This worksheet analyzes five factors in tray interpretation. The five areas are: Vision (i.e., problem statement, resources, and obstacles); Emotion (i.e., expression of emotion in the client and the related emotional state of the therapist); Relationship (i.e., co-transference variables and possible symbolic representation); Dynamics (i.e., themes, manifestations of the psyche, or self-symbols); and Organization (i.e., regulated/disregulated states, space, degree of water use, elements represented, what type of representation of the client's struggles).

c. Sandplay Therapy Session Note: This note was adapted from a more generic session note for Medicaid clients written up by Sandplay teaching member Karen Wheeler (personal communication). The format includes billing codes; treatment goals; recently reported behavioral symptoms; present client mood, energy levels, cognitive state, and behaviors; session modalities used; client play themes; and session content, in terms of client response to therapy and participation.

In my workshops teaching supervisors and consultants, I request that they familiarize themselves with individual and/or group consultation facilitator guidelines as well. There are other forms I encourage trainees to begin to use and discuss in consultation, depending on whether the therapist is a supervisor trainee or case presenter:

a. A background form for therapists interested in individual and/or group sandplay;
b. Individual and/or group consultation presentation guidelines;
c. Individual and/or group consultation facilitator guidelines;
d. An authorization form filled out by parents, guardians of the child or teen, or an adult client. This form formalizes consent to allow case material to be used with identifying information removed before presenting in a group or at a regional or national conference, using the therapist's own name or logo.

The individual therapist can then gather information about the trays and proceed to fill out the forms found on page 34 for case presentation.

a. The first question therapists need to answer before using the Sandplay Journey Map is: Has the client actually "Answered the Call," and chosen to journey? If yes, the following forms can be used to further this process of analyzing and interpreting case material.
b. Tray Description and Sandplay Therapy Session Note Forms assist therapists to more thoroughly document session details (e.g., diagramming the movement and placement of symbols) for later consultation and/or presentation.
c. A Sandplay Naming Sheet allows the therapist the option of arranging the individual sandtrays for each session over the progression of trays, as noted earlier on p. 66.
d. Employing the Sandplay Journey Map: Tray Distribution Form: Here therapists begin to group the trays within gateways. The trays can be organized by which of the four elements (fire, water, air, and earth, or any element system) are present and combined through tracking the progress of the client's journey through

the mandala of the journey as well as exploring the progression of self-symbols throughout the child's process.

e. The final step asks the trainees to consider the information about the client they have compiled, and fill out a Case Presentation Background sheet to help them formulate how they'd like to organize their case presentation for use in individual or group consultation activities.

## Some Thoughts on How to Handle Mistakes: It's All Grist for the Mill

When we first start working with the Sandplay Journey Map, we begin to look over the child's work in its entirety—including our co-transference and responses in general. As we go over this material, we may find that we have made mistakes that we need to process with a supervisor or in consultation, either in a group or individually. At workshops and conferences, the sandplay teacher frequently offers the finest examples of their work in the hope that will provide the best case demonstration and effect. This can create an unrealistic expectation that the process will go without any obstacles—which can become opportunities for professional and personal growth. When engaging in sandplay consultation, in addition to asking for assistance with enlarging our understanding of a client case, we need to build in experience by sharing our perceived mistakes and sometimes even our failures with families, and our attendant feelings of vulnerability and shame.

I have found it is when I make mistakes, when I forget to listen carefully to a client, that I learn the most in mindfully managing the aftermath. For example, I mishandled a sandplay session with a child working out severe anxiety issues. Lina and her mother experienced a number of school staff trying to compel Lina's cooperation verbally, and sometimes physically. After the first few sessions, when Lina tentatively moved the sand around with her fingers, she entered the sandplay room eagerly, allowing her mother to stay in the waiting room. Lina began to gather objects to place in the dry tray. She whirled around, and her energy level heightened. From my seated position, she appeared to "dump" the contents of container after container of stones, gems, and flowers into the tray. I let my anxiety get in the way of her tray-making. I got up and interrupted her, speaking softly but firmly. "Before you keep going, I'd like to see what you're doing," I remember saying. She stopped immediately and looked up at me, surprised. As I got closer and peered into the tray, I saw a lovely pattern emerging in the sand. This was no random or chaotic figure dumping. I had just blown it, in sandplay terms, by interfering with her tray-making. This could easily have negative consequences for our relationship as well.

Lina looked away, and wouldn't maintain eye contact at all. She drooped. I immediately apologized to her, as gently as I could, for questioning what she had put together. And I added that I wanted to let her mom know that I had made a mistake, without telling specifically anything that Lina herself had done (so as not to break the relational container between therapist and client). That meant, I explained to Lina, that I would say I had asked too many questions and hadn't just let Lina do what she needed to do. I believed that with her history of being mishandled and misunderstood, this piece of making that apology more "public," was necessary. She just stared at me, then nodded once, very slightly. After my apology, she indicated silently that she wanted to leave the session. I asked her to think about whether she would come back, with the idea that I had made a mistake and was going to make sure I learned from it. She quickly walked ahead of me into the waiting room. I told her mother I had made a mistake, while Lina listened and looked to the side.

The next time I saw her, Lina still didn't look directly at me, and silently drew for the next hour. The session after that, she went right to the sand. Lina glanced up at me. Once. I was being given another chance. As I believe every interaction in the office is "grist for the mill," I moved on with Lina, knowing I had some strong work to do to acknowledge my anxiety, my shortcomings in this area, and work through that in my own therapy and supervision sessions. As one of my colleagues, Miho Katsumata of Japan, softly mused, "We don't know when the moment comes" (personal communication, 2016). I found in mapping Lina's journey that she began exhibiting more confident behaviors outwardly and with regard to her trays from then on. Lina knew with more surety that she would have a more attentive and respectful therapist, and her sand stories demonstrated this renewed energy in the vitality of her heroines. I know whatever that defining moment, it is important to be prepared for it as mindfully as possible. It feels good to offer up such an opportunity as this for reflection with other therapists as well.

# PART VI

~

# CONCLUSIONS

Perhaps real wisdom lies in not seeking answers at all. Any answer we find will not be true for long. An answer is a place where we can fall asleep as life moves past us to its next question. After all these years I have begun to wonder if the secret of living well is not in having all the answers but in pursuing unanswerable questions in good company.

Rachel Naomi Remen,
"Mystery," *My Grandfather's Blessings*, p. 338 (2001)
Reprinted with permission

# CHAPTER ELEVEN

~

# Finding Our Way Home

Using the Journey Map is a means to more fully appreciate the healing and often transformative journeys of my clients, the girls who face unbearable suffering at times. There is no absolute way to understand the constructions, symbolism, or the myth-making of sandplay—what literally lies before us in the trays are "unanswerable questions" that we regard with awe in the excellent company of other sandplay enthusiasts and colleagues.

Therapy is a serious business, literally and metaphorically. Therapists and counselors are taught vital ethics, relationship considerations and boundaries, and discernment in implementing best-practice strategies and modalities. And yet . . . the value of the relationship in therapeutic work—and the resonance of this word "work" is hugely important—lies in our mindful lending of presence and experience as we accompany our clients to transform suffering and discomfort into meaningful perspective-taking and practice. Therapists using the Sandplay Journey Map can more comfortably track and analyze their clients' progress in sandplay. And isn't lightening our burden as responsible therapists in an easeful and understandable way a wonderful thing?

Rachel Simmons says, "The most precious gift we can give girls is the liberty not only to listen to the greater voice of themselves but to act on it. This is the simplest kind of freedom and the most sacred sort of empowerment" (2009, p. 253).

I talked about writing this book with a young girl in the context of sharing our fears about tackling new skills. Marika remarked that "I want to make a tray to show other people who play with kids in the sand room what it's all about." I call her tray "The Solving Point." She described her tray:

> It looks like a huge thing. If anybody came in, put in one thing, it could symbolize everybody's problems and how it was solved, showing that everybody has a problem and it has a solving point. I didn't know that before I came back [to see me in therapy again]. I figured that out. If you're afraid, it's a huge problem. The pink pearls and

purple pearls represent big problems; the smaller things can be fixed more easily. I put trust in the middle.

When we choose to face our fears, to reach for more, we become stronger, clearer, and highly engaged in living fully. Sandplay makes the journey bearable and allows our hearts to open to what is possible for us in each moment. We aim to stand next to our clients, our arm metaphorically around their shoulders, gazing hopefully into the panorama of the tray in front of them. We have the tools to scrutinize this journey in depth, to whatever place they find themselves drawn, within the temenos of the therapeutic container. What wonderful adventures we will have . . .

# APPENDIX

~

# Some Important Sandplay Definitions

*Archetype:* An archetype in Jungian theory can be explained as the matrix of potential, expansive, universal energy which comes from the collective unconscious to consciousness. The term *collective unconscious* can mean the stored and shared material from the history of all cultures, ethnicities, and groups of humans. Archetypal representations of fundamental patterns of human experience exist outside of time and space. When an archetype manifests in repeating patterns, themes, images, or symbols through either the individual or collective psyche, behaviors and actions of the possibilities of the archetypal energy are revealed in unlimited ways (Jung, 1968). Jung theorized that "the archetypes have, when they appear, a distinctly numinous character, which can only be described as 'spiritual,' if 'magical' is too strong a word" (1970, p. 115). In this sense, the "numinous" is that which is deeply felt, something sacred and transcendent, connected to the divine.

The best way to understand archetypes is through metaphor. This illustrative story is about Moses, the beloved of God, savior and hero of the Jewish people. Moses knew that the Israelites had, so to speak, "blown it" when they erected a statue of Baal and worshipped it during their exodus. Through encountering the presence of God at the Tent of Meeting, the prophet bargained with God to show himself and not abandon the people after their faithless behavior. In fact, Moses proved himself a "nudge" (in Yiddish, someone who pushes and pushes his point) without letup. Finally, God agreed to show himself, but warned Moses of the potential harm. God told Moses to stand in the shelter of a cleft in a rock nearby. God would pass by the rock, and the Shadow of God would fall upon Moses. God's hand would protect and screen Moses, since no one can see God's countenance and live. Indeed, when this came to pass, Moses ran raving in the desert for 40 days and 40 nights in spiritual ecstasy. The power of the archetype of God was too great to be experienced firsthand.

*Centering:* Trays that begin to show wholeness; self-symbols that are used in patterns in an increasingly circular fashion.

*Constellation of the self:* Trays that manifest in the numinous, showing the client's perception of the "light" and beauty in their inner sense of being, symbolizing "the treasure within."

*"Free and protected space":* Kalff talked about using the temenos to create this relational and sacred space between client and therapist. Initially, she used the term *sheltered* as well as *protected* to define this term. Therapists are to provide a nonjudgmental, witnessing, and observing attitude in the play room and act as guardians of the client's freedom of expression and demonstration of their psyche's needs and journeys through the sandtrays and verbalizations.

*Individuation:* In the book *Individuation in Fairy Tales*, Marie-Louise von Franz spoke of

> the term which C. G. Jung describes the psychological process of inner growth and centralization by which the individual finds its own self. This does not mean to find one's own ego-identity, as is described by many modern psychological schools. By the term *self*, Jung understands an ultimately unknowable inner center of the total personality and also the totality itself. This center can only be approached but never integrated. Our destiny and our health depend on it. In the various religions and mythologies it is symbolized by the image of the "treasure hard to attain," the mandala and all images of the inner psychic manifestation of the godhead.

*Return to the collective:* Grounding oneself in reality, in returning "home" from a wounded place and taking the newfound wisdom and treasure back to where we live, as demonstrated in trays that use more of the figures and symbolism of daily routine and life and bring new perspective.

*Self/Ego:* The psyche consists of the conscious and unconscious, and the interaction between them. It has a drive toward wholeness and has a tendency to balance itself through the compensatory function of the unconscious. The realization of wholeness (self) suggests that the psyche, like the body, has the ability to attempt to heal itself. The self is the totality (both the conscious and unconscious aspects) of the personality and is its directing center. It organizes the psyche, and the ego evolves from it. This is the ego-self axis, and connects between our heart and mind when we allow wisdom to enter. The autonomy of the ego is limited since its roots are in the unconscious. The ego is vulnerable to influence by emotionally charged complexes acting in a compensatory way. The more it tries to control or suppress, the more the complex will rob the ego of control.

*Shadow:*

> That part of ourselves that we are not ready to bring into consciousness, which we deny or is as yet unknown or unincorporated into our psyche. The shadow refers to that internal material that we either don't want to face, aren't ready to know about

ourselves, or aren't yet capable of understanding and integrating. It doesn't have to do with concepts of evil, really, just those darker denied aspects of ourselves to which we aren't yet reconciled (Heiko, 2010).

*Temenos:* The therapist creates a predictable, nonjudgmental, and safe environment that allows the person a space to freely express themselves. The therapist creates safety by protecting the person's privacy, honoring their uniqueness, and at the same time defining the limits of the "holding" space. The therapist must be prepared to accept the person's shadow material, allowing for its identification, integration, and incorporation into the psyche of the client.

*The role of the therapist in the symbolic process:* "Engaging in the process of coming to understand" through maintaining an open and observing attitude. The therapist would not presume to know what the client is feeling or thinking; that is expressed symbolically and freely, without interpretation by the therapist over the tray in any manner.

*Tension of the opposites:* "The term *tension of the opposites* refers to the dynamic and often ambivalent strain between two aspects of our nature, our yearnings, our needs—such as love and hate or a belief in one's essential goodness versus one's feelings of worthlessness or inadequacy" (Heiko, 2010, p. 174). Jung believed that the psyche was a manifestation of the life force. This energy was seen as being generated by the opposites contained and reflected in the two poled aspect of the archetype (e.g., the nurturing Mother versus the devouring Mother). This tension can represent that which we are drawn to, and that which we fear most. Often, we believe that we cannot live with nor accept both elements, issues, or conflicts as existing within us at the same time. We are caught in the middle of this unconscious material and dynamic tension between what we want most and of which we are most afraid.

*Transcendent function:* In order to bridge conscious and unconscious processes in the psyche, this function creates a dialogue in a unique way to allow something "other" to emerge, something that is involved in the aspect of the self-regulating nature of the processes involved in individuation, the psyche as a while, and the integration of the self in the drive toward unity and wholeness.

# References

Afanesev, A., and Alexeieff, A. (trans. Norbert Guterman). (1973). *Russian Fairy Tales: The Pantheon Fairy Tale and Folktale Library*. New York: Pantheon.

Amatruda, K., and Helm Simpson, P. (2008). *Sandplay: The Sacred Healing: A Guide to Symbolic Process*. http://psychceu.com/Sandplaybookpage1.asp

Arrien, A. (2007). *The Second Half of Life: Opening the Eight Gates of Wisdom*. Louisville, CO: Sounds True.

Babyatsky-Grayson, D. E. (2014). "Counseling Transgender Youth Utilizing the Expressive Art Therapies." Doctoral dissertation, American Academy of Clinical Sexologists.

Bales, R. (2001). *The Cambridge Companion to Proust* (Cambridge Companions to Literature). Cambridge, UK: Cambridge University Press.

Berra, Y. (2001). *When You Come to a Fork in the Road, Take It!: Inspiration and Wisdom from One of Baseball's Greatest Heroes*. New York: Hachette.

Bettleheim, B. (2010). *The Uses of Enchantment: The Meaning and Importance of Fairy Tales*. New York: Vintage.

Blythe, S. S. quoted in Baldwin, C. (1990). *Life's Companion: Journal Writing as a Spiritual Quest*. New York: Bantam Books.

Bradway, K., and McCoard, B. (1997). *Sandplay: Silent Workshop of the Psyche*. New York: Routledge.

Breslau, J., Gilman, S., Stein, B., Ruder, T., Gmelin, R., and Miller, E. (May 30, 2017). "Sex Differences in Recent First-Onset Depression in an Epidemiological Sample of Adolescents," *Translational Psychiatry* 7, e1139; doi:10.1038/tp.2017.105. Published online May 30, 2017.

Bridges, E. M. (2011). "Innocence Found: A Review of Working with Children to Heal Interpersonal Trauma: The Power of Play by Eliana Gil (ed.)." *Psych Critiques*, 56(7), *Contemporary Psychology*, APA Review of Books February 16, 2011.

Brill, S. A., and Pepper, R. (2008). *The Transgender Child: A Handbook for Families and Professionals*. Berkeley, CA: Cleis.

Brock, M. A. (2014). "Reflections: Books and Events Journal of Sandplay Therapy" for Cunningham, L., "The Psyche Knows Best: An Interview of Florence Swan Porter Grossenbacher," *Journal of Sandplay Therapy* (online).

Bull, J., in Radner, G. (1989). *It's Always Something*. New York: Simon & Schuster.

Campbell, J. (2008). *Hero with a Thousand Faces*. Novato, CA: New World Library.

Chevalier, J., and Gheerbrant, A. (trans. John Buchanan-Brown). (1997). *The Penguin Dictionary of Symbols*. London: Penguin.

Cirlot, J. E. (2014). *A Dictionary of Symbols*. New York: Welcome Rain.

Clift, J. D. and Clift, W. B. (1991). *The Hero Journey in Dreams*. New York: Crossroad Publishing Company.

Cohen-Sandler, R. (2005). *Stressed-out Girls: Helping Them Thrive in the Age of Pressure*. New York: Viking.

Cunningham, L. (2013). *Sandplay and the Clinical Relationship*. San Francisco: Sempervirens.

Drewes, A. A., Bratton, S. C., and Schaefer, C. E. (2011). *Integrative Play Therapy*. Amazon Digital Services.

Dundes, A. (ed.). (1986). *Cinderella: A Casebook*. Madison: University of Wisconsin Press.

Engelsman, J. (1993). *The Queen's Cloak: A Myth for Mid-life*. Asheville, NC: Chiron.

Estes, C. P. (1992). *Women Who Run with the Wolves: Myths and Stories of the Wild Woman Archetype*. New York: Ballantine Books.

Frankel, V. E. (2010). *From Girl to Goddess: The Heroine's Journey through Myth and Legend*. Jefferson, NC: McFarland.

Friedman, H. and Mitchell, R. R. (1994). *Sandplay: Past, Present and Future*. New York: Routledge.

Gil, E. (2009). *Helping Abused and Traumatized Children: Integrating Directive and Nondirective Approaches*. New York: Guilford.

Goldman, L. (2014). "Integrating Expressive Arts and Research-Supported Play-Based Interventions with LGBTQI Adolescents." In Green, E. J., and Myrick, A. C. (eds.), *Play Therapy with Vulnerable Populations: No Child Forgotten*. Lanham, MD: Rowman & Littlefield.

Green, E. J. (2014). *The Handbook of Jungian Play Therapy with Children and Adolescents*. Baltimore, MD: Johns Hopkins University Press.

Green, E. J., and Myrick, A. C. (2014). "Treating Complex Trauma in Adolescents: A Phase-Based, Integrative Approach for Play Therapists," *International Journal of Play Therapy*, 23(3).

Green, E. J., Myrick, A. C., and Crenshaw, D. A. (2013). "Toward Secure Attachment in Adolescent Relational Development: Advancements from Sandplay and Expressive Play-Based Interventions," *International Journal of Play Therapy*, 22(2).

Grubbs, G. (2005). *The Sandplay Categorical Checklist for Sandplay Analysis*. Auckland, New Zealand: Rubedo.

Hains, R. C. (2014). *The Princess Problem: Guiding Our Girls through the Princess-Obsessed Years*. Naperville, IL: Sourcebooks.

Heiko, R. L. (2004). "Children's Birthday Party Sandplays," *Journal of Sandplay Therapy*, 13(2).

———. (2008). "Finding the Treasure Within: The Sandplay Journey of Stella," *Journal of Sandplay Therapy*, 17(1).

———. (2010). *Working with Children to Heal Interpersonal Trauma: The Power of Play*. New York: Guilford.

———. (2015). "Tempered in the Fire: Self-Care and Mindfulness in Preventing Clinical Burnout." In Green, E. J., Baggerly, J. N., and Myrick, A. C. (eds.), *Counseling Families: Play-Based Treatment*. Lanham, MD: Rowman & Littlefield.

Hirschfield, J. (2015). "Living by Questions," *O Magazine*. June 12.

Hogarth, R. (2001). *Educating Intuition*. Chicago, IL: University of Chicago Press.

Homeyer, L. E. (2010). *Sandtray Therapy: A Practical Manual* (2nd ed). London: Routledge.

Hunter, L. B. (1998). *Images of Resiliency: Troubled Children Create Healing Stories in the Language of Sandplay*. Palm Beach, FL: Behavioral Communications Institute.

Jung, C. G. (ed. Aniela Jaffe) (trans. Clara Winston). (1965). *Memories, Dreams and Reflections*. New York: Vintage.

———. (trans. Gerhard Adler and R. F. C. Hull). (1966). "The Practice of Psychotherapy." In *The Collected Works of C. G. Jung*, Vol. 16. Princeton, NJ: Princeton University Press.

———. (1968). "Archetypes and the Collective Unconscious." In *The Collected Works of C. G. Jung*, Vol. 9(1). New York: Routledge.

———. (trans. Gerhard Adler and R. F. C. Hull). (1970). "Structure and Dynamics of the Psyche." In *The Collected Works of C. G. Jung*, Vol. 8. Princeton, NJ: Princeton University Press.

———. (1968). *Man and His Symbols*. New York: Dell.

———. (trans. Gerhard Adler and R. F. C. Hull). (1977). "Mysterium Coniunctionis." In *The Collected Works of C. G. Jung*, Vol. 14. Princeton, NJ: Princeton University Press.

———. (trans. Gerhard Adler and R.F.C. Hull). (1983). "Aspects of the Feminine," from Vols. 6, 7, 9i, 9ii, 10, 17, *Collected Works)* (Jung Extracts). Princeton, NJ: Princeton University Press.

———. (1983). *The Psychology of the Transference*. New York: Routledge.

———. (2014). *Four Archetypes*. London: Routledge.

Kalff, D. M. (2004). *Sandplay: A Psychotherapeutic Approach to the Psyche*. Cloverdale, CA: Temenos.

Kalff, M. (2013). "Experience Related Case Study: Like a Masked Ball?" *Journal of Sandplay Therapy*, 22(2).

Kaplan, J., Punnett, A., and Zappacosta, J. (2009). "Sandplay Therapy with Children: Talking with Parents," *Journal of Sandplay Therapy*, 18(2).

Koch, C. (May 1, 2015). "Intuition May Reveal Where Expertise Resides in the Brain," *Scientific American*. Retrieved from https://www.scientificamerican.com/article/intuition-may-reveal-where-expertise-resides-in-the-brain/

Kornfield, J. (2014). *A Lamp in the Darkness: Illuminating the Path through Difficult Times*. Boulder, CO: Sounds True.

Labovitz Boik, B., and Goodwin, E. A. (2000). *Sandplay Therapy: A Step-by-Step Manual for Psychotherapists of Diverse Orientations* (Norton Professional Books). New York: W. W. Norton.

Loue, S. (2012). "Sandplay Therapy: Identity, Diversity, and Cultural Humility," *Journal of Sandplay Therapy*, 21(2).

Lowenfeld, M. (1979). *The World Technique*. London: Allen & Unwin.

Mayer, M. (1994). *Baba Yaga and Vasilisa the Brave*. New York: HarperCollins.

McMillan, I. (2015). "The Sword, the Pen, and the Arrow: Transforming Disciplines through Disciplines," Waldorf Today, http://www.waldorftoday.com/2015/06/the-sword-the-pen-and-the-arrow-transforming-disciplines-through-disciplines.

Metcalf, S. (November 4, 2007). "Town without Pity," *New York Times*. November 4 [Accessed www.nytimes.com on Noember 14, 2015]

Metzger, D., quoted in Simms, L. (2011). *Our Secret Territory: The Essence of Storytelling*. Boulder, CO: Sentient.

Mitchell, R. R., and Friedman, H. (2017). "Archetypal Themes in the Sandplay Process," *Journal of Sandplay Therapy*, 26(1).

Murdock, M. (1990). *The Heroine's Journey: Woman's Quest for Wholeness*. Boulder, CO: Shambhala.

Neumann, E. (2015). *The Great Mother: An Analysis of the Archetype*, trans. Ralph Manheim. Princeton, NJ: Princeton University Press.

Olofsdotter, M. (2007). *Sofia and the Heartmender*. Duluth, MN: Holy Cow! Press.

Olson-Morrison, D. (2017). "Integrative Play Therapy with Adults with Complex Trauma: A Developmentally-Informed Approach," *International Journal of Play Therapy*, Vol. 26(3).

Olson, K. R., Durwood, L., DeMeules, M., and McLaughlin, K. A. Elaine (2016). "Mental Health of Transgender Children Who Are Supported in Their Identities," *Pediatrics*, 137(3).

Orenstein, P. (2012). *Cinderella Ate My Daughter: Dispatches from the Front Lines of the New Girlie-Girl Culture*. New York: HarperCollins.

Paddleford, J., quoted in Alexander, K., and Harris, C. (2009). *Hometown Appetites: The Story of Clementine Paddleford, the Forgotten Food Writer Who Chronicled How America Ate*. New York: Penguin/Random House.

Pastore, V. L. (2007). "Masculine Initiation: The Stages of Sandplay of Younger Men and Boys," *Journal of Sandplay Therapy*, 16(2).

Pattis Zoja, E. (2004). *Sandplay Therapy: Treatment of Psychopathologies: Understanding with the Hands*. [Kindle DX version.]

Pearson, M., and Wilson, H. (2001). *Sandplay and Symbol Work: Emotional Healing and Personal Development with Children, Adolescents and Adults*. Camberwell, Australia: Acer.

Pilinovsky, H. (2004). "Russian Fairy Tales: Baba Yaga's Domain," *Journal of Mythic Arts*. http://endicottstudio.typepad.com/articleslist/baba-yagas-domain-by-helen-pilinovsky.html

Pipher, M. (2005). *Reviving Ophelia: Saving the Selves of Adolescent Girls*. New York: Riverhead.

Pratchett, T. (2009). *Carpe Jugulum: A Novel of Discworld*. New York: HarperCollins.

Rae, R. (2015). *Sandtray: Playing to Heal, Recover, and Grow*. Lanham, MD: Rowman & Littlefield.

Remen, R. N. (2001). *My Grandfather's Blessings: Stories of Strength, Refuge, and Belonging*. New York: Riverhead Books.

Rich, A. (2002). *The Fact of a Doorframe: Poems 1950–2001*. New York: W. W. Norton.

Ryce-Menuhin, J. (1992, reprinted 2014). *Jungian Sandplay: The Wonderful Therapy*. New York: Routledge.

Shantideva (trans. Georg Feuerstein). (1970). *Entering the Path of Enlightenment*. Tucson, AZ: Integral.

Siegel, D. J. (2015). *The Developing Mind* (2nd ed.): *How Relationships and the Brain Interact to Shape Who We Are*. New York: Guilford.

Siegel, D. J. and Bryson, T. P. (2012). *The Whole-Brain Child: 12 Revolutionary Strategies to Nurture Your Child's Developing Mind*. New York: Bantam Books.

Signell, K. A. (1990). *Wisdom of the Heart: Working with Women's Dreams*. New York: Bantam.

Simmons, R. (2009). *The Curse of the Good Girl: Raising Authentic Girls with Courage and Confidence*. New York: Penguin.

———. (2011). *Odd Girl Out, Revised and Updated: The Hidden Culture of Aggression in Girls*. New York: Mariner.

Singer, J. (1994). *Boundaries of the Soul: The Practice of Jung's Psychology*. New York: Anchor Books.

Spitz, E. H. (2015). "The Irresistible Psychology of Fairy Tales." https://newrepublic.com/article/126582/irresistible-psychology-fairy-tales, December 28.

Steiber, E. (2007). "Brother and Sister: A Matter of Seeing," *Journal of Mythic Arts*. http://www.endicott-studio.com/articleslist/brother-and-sister-a-matter-of-seeing-by-ellen-steiber.html

Stein, M. (1995). *Psyche's Stories: Modern Jungian Interpretations of Fairy Tales* (Book 3). Asheville, NC: Chiron.

Steinhardt, L. (2000). *Foundation and Form in Jungian Sandplay*. London: Jessica Kingsley.

Tatar, M. (2002). *The Annotated Classic Fairy Tales*. New York: W. W. Norton.

Thomas, B. (2011). *Play and Art Therapy Interventions for Gender Nonconforming Children and Their Families*. Unpublished manusript.

Tolle, E. (2010). *The Power of Now: A Guide to Spiritual Enlightenment*. Novato, CA: New World Library. [Kindle DX version.] Retrieved from amazon.com.

van der Kolk, B. (2014). *The Body Keeps the Score: Brain, Mind, and Body in the Healing of Trauma*. New York: Viking. [Kindle DX version.] Retrieved from amazon.com.

von Franz, M-L. (1995). *Shadow and Evil in Fairy Tales*. Boulder, CO: Shambhala.

———. (1996). *The Interpretation of Fairy Tales*. Boulder, CO: Shambhala.

———. (1972). *The Feminine in Fairytales*. Dallas, TX: Spring Publications, Inc.

von Gontard, A. (2011). "The Numinous in Sandplay Therapy with Children and Adolescents," *Journal of Sandplay Therapy*, 20(2).

Wallis, L. (1985). "Prologue: The Three Lessons." In *Stories for the Third Ear: Using Hypnotic Fables in Psychology*. New York: W. W. Norton.

Warner, M. (2014). *Once Upon a Time: A Short History of Fairy Tale*. New York: Oxford University Press.

Weinrib, E. L. (2004). *Images of the Self: The Sandplay Therapy Process*. Cloverdale, CA: Temenos.

Winerman, L. (2005). "What We Know Without Knowing How," *APA Monitor*, 36(3), 50.

Wiseman, R. (2016). *Queen Bees and Wannabes* (3rd ed.): *Helping Your Daughter Survive Cliques, Gossip, Boys, and the New Realities of Girl World*. New York: Harmony.

# Index

Page references for figures are italicized.

~

# About the Author

Psychologist **Rosalind Heiko**, PhD, NCSP, RPT-S, ISST (aka Dr. Roz), is a Registered Play Therapist-Supervisor and Sandplay Teacher. She believes wholeheartedly in the power of laughter and the delight that sandplay brings to her clients and trainees. Dr. Roz has worked with children, adolescents, and families professionally since 1983. She is the director of Pediatric & Family Psychology, P.A., in Cary, North Carolina, and travels around the world to train therapists working with children and families. In addition to her practice and training, Dr. Roz is an author. Dr. Roz's chapter, "Tempered in the Fire: Self-Care & Mindfulness in Preventing Clinical Burn-Out," can be found in *Counseling Families: Play-Based Treatment*. She is a highly regarded contributor to the *Journal of Sandplay Therapy*. Dr. Roz is the founder of NC Sandplay Training and a past board of trustees member of the Sandplay Therapists of America. She is an Approved Teaching Consultant in Clinical Hypnosis (ASCH), is Level II certified in EMDR, and holds national certification in school psychology (NCSP). Visit her at www.drheiko.com.

www.ingramcontent.com/pod-product-compliance
Lightning Source LLC
Chambersburg PA
CBHW051425290326
41932CB00048B/3217